Computer Aided
Legal Research

The West Legal Studies Series

Your options keep growing with West Legal Studies

Each year our list continues to offer you more options for every area of the law to meet your course or on-the-job reference requirements. We now have over 140 titles from which to choose in the following areas:

Administrative Law	Family Law
Alternative Dispute Resolution	Federal Taxation
Bankruptcy	Intellectual Property
Business Organizations/Corporations	Introduction to Law
Civil Litigation and Procedure	Introduction to Paralegalism
CLA Exam Preparation	Law Office Management
Client Accounting	Law Office Procedures
Computer in the Law Office	Legal Research, Writing, and Analysis
Constitutional Law	Legal Terminology
Contract Law	Paralegal Employment
Criminal Law and Procedure	Real Estate Law
Document Preparation	Reference Materials
Environmental Law	Torts and Personal Injury Law
Ethics	Will, Trusts, and Estate Administration

You will find unparalleled, practical support

Each book is augmented by instructor and student supplements to ensure the best learning experience possible. We also offer custom publishing and other benefits such as West's Student Achievement Award. In addition, our sales representatives are ready to provide you with dependable service.

We want to hear from you

Our best contributions for improving the quality of our books and instructional materials is feedback from the people who use them. If you have a question, concern, or observation about any of our materials, or you have a product proposal or manuscript, we want to hear from you. Please contact your local representative or write us at the following address:

West Legal Studies, 5 Maxwell Drive, P.O. Box 8007, Clifton Park, NY 12065

For additional information point your browser at

www.westlegalstudies.com

THOMSON

DELMAR LEARNING

Computer Aided Legal Research

JUDY A. LONG, J.D.

THOMSON

DELMAR LEARNING

Australia   Canada   Mexico   Singapore   Spain   United Kingdom   United States

THOMSON

DELMAR LEARNING

WEST LEGAL STUDIES

Computer Aided Legal Research
Judy A. Long, J.D.

Business Unit Director:
Susan L. Simpfenderfer

Executive Editor:
Marlene McHugh Pratt

Senior Acquisitions Editor:
Joan M. Gill

Editorial Assistant:
Lisa Flatley

Executive Production Manager:
Wendy A. Troeger

Production Manager:
Carolyn Miller

Production Editor:
Betty L. Dickson

Executive Marketing Manager:
Donna J. Lewis

Channel Manager:
Nigar Hale

Cover Image:
ARTVILLE, LLC.

For permission to use material from this text or product, contact us by
Tel (800) 730-2214
Fax (800) 730-2215
www.thomsonrights.com

Library of Congress Cataloging-in-Publication Data

Long, Judy A., 1937–
    Computer aided legal research/Judy A. Long.
        p. cm. — (The West Legal Studies series)
    Includes index.
    ISBN 0-7668-1333-9
    1. Legal research—United States—Computer network resources. 2. Legal research—United States—Data processing. 3. Information storage and retrieval systems—Law—United States. 4. Internet. I. Title. II. Series.

KF242.A1 L655 2003
340'.07'2073—dc21
                                                    2002025607

NOTICE TO THE READER

TO BILL

CONTENTS

Any attempt to address all aspects of computer-aided legal research in one textbook is a tremendous task. This book is divided into chapters on the various forms of legal research accessible by using the computer. It begins with a brief explanation of computers and a short chapter on manual research, a topic that is usually covered in a separate course in most legal programs.

Internet research is becoming increasingly popular as computers become faster and easier to operate and as the sites available become more meaningful for the legal professional. The search process is discussed and various search engines are explained. The terminology used on the Internet is defined in each chapter and also in the glossary. Many different Web sites are listed, as well as explanations of their practical usage in the law office.

Chapters on general and legal uses of the Internet are included in the text. The most commonly used feature of the Internet, e-mail, is defined and explained. Methods of using the Internet for factual research are discussed, including finding people and businesses, conducting meetings online, obtaining travel information, and finding locations by using various mapping services.

Many comprehensive sites provide links to other legal sources. Often a search begins with one of these sources, such as FindLaw. The federal government maintains many sites for government agencies, federal courts, federal court opinions, and federal statutes. The states offer a number of sites for their government offices, cases, and statutes.

Secondary sources are easily accessible. Most law schools and their law libraries offer links to other valuable sites. Various law firms offer their own sites with links to various legal topics. Chapter 9 outlines the sites for specialized areas of the law.

Considerable material is provided on the Westlaw® system, including obtaining subscriptions, getting online, and conducting searches. The LEXIS® system and its organization is introduced. CD-ROM systems are described, as well as the Loislaw® online system, which offers CDs as well.

Unique features of this text include a glossary of terms, end-of-chapter review questions, and practical problems that are similar to those that would be encountered in a law office. Practical examples are given throughout the text for the circumstances under which each system and/or Web site is used. Helpful hints are provided for using the various sources described.

Acknowledgments

Many individuals provided assistance in the preparation of this textbook. I would like to thank Joan Gill, editor, Lisa Flatley, assistant editor, Betty L. Dickson, production editor, and Sharon Green, copyeditor, for their help and guidance throughout the writing process.

The following individuals provided valuable suggestions and ideas for improvement of the text in their reviews:

Ruth Stevens
Davenport College

David Jaroszewski
Lee College

Laurel Vietzen
Elgin Community College

Regina Judge
Montclair State University

Carol Andary
Lake Superior State University

I would also like to thank Louie Adame, who assisted in the revisions and updating of the material on LEXIS.

A special thanks to all of the individuals who enabled me to feature pictures of their Web pages in the text, and to all who I may have inadvertently omitted.

Judy A. Long, J.D.

Please note that the Internet resources are of a time-sensitive nature and URL addresses may often change or be deleted.

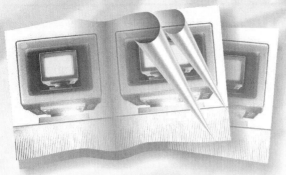

CHAPTER 1

Legal Research

INTRODUCTION

Computer-assisted legal research (CALR) enables you to perform legal research at your computer terminal. It includes using the Internet, various CD-ROM systems on the market, Westlaw®, LEXIS, and other available systems for legal research. No text on legal research using the computer would be complete without a detailed analysis of manual legal research as well. In many cases, a combination of manual and computer research is advantageous, particularly in those situations where the user is performing complex research using one of the subscription services, such as Westlaw or LEXIS.

In order to save on expenses, some law offices will instruct the researcher to initially perform manual research using law books or research via the Internet. These forms of research are done without incurring additional expense. Once the major issues are framed and preparatory material is obtained, the researcher may then log on to one of the subscription services, which generally charge a per-minute fee while connected to the service.

As computers become easier to operate, more people enjoy working with them. Law office personnel are finding that complicated research, which would take several hours manually, takes only minutes using the computer. Increased usage in law firms can be attributed to the decreased cost of computers as well as to their ease of use.

The focus of this text is to discuss the specific uses of the computer for legal research. However, many paralegals perform considerable factual research using the Internet, CD-ROM systems, and LEXIS or Westlaw. Therefore, the use of these systems in that context will be described.

BASIC TERMS

Computers process and store information. In order to operate a computer, one must have a keyboard for inputting information, a central processing unit for processing data, a monitor for viewing data, and a mouse or other pointing device. The operator usually enters information into the computer via the keyboard or mouse. However, scanners and voice-recognition software are also being used for this purpose. The monitor provides visual output of data stored in the computer. This output information may then be copied to a printer or placed in a file on the hard drive for later retrieval. Once the file has been saved on the hard drive or a diskette, the information may be sent to others as an attachment to e-mail, via a fax machine, or by regular mail.

USING THE INTERNET

One method for sending material to another computer is through the Internet via e-mail. E-mail allows the sender to compose and send messages as well as attachments. Messages are sent instantly to recipients all over the world. Many people prefer this method of communication over telephone calls as it avoids the problem of playing "telephone tag." E-mail eliminates the use of paper and postage and allows for quicker responses to questions, statements, or documents.

The user must have a modem and a subscription with an Internet service provider in order to use this e-mail service. Most service providers enable the subscriber to connect to the Internet via a local telephone number, thereby avoiding the expense of a long-distance call. E-mail may be sent to other parts of the country or world without incurring telephone charges for more than a local telephone call.

Cable services use special lines and are generally provided by television cable companies. Modems are not needed for cable services since a special cable is installed. Monthly service charges are billed to the user.

Most service providers charge a flat monthly fee with no additional charges for time spent online. A few companies do charge by the number of hours spent online. However, a flat monthly fee is the preferred method of billing for Internet service.

Westlaw and LEXIS have contracts that charge for the amount of time you are connected to their service while you are online; they also provide flat monthly fee contracts. These rates vary depending on the type of services required. Access to their databases may be obtained through the Internet or through a special program using a modem.

MANUAL RESEARCH

The traditional method of doing legal research has always been using books from the law library. Publications may be found for cases, statutes, treatises, digests, manuals, indexes, encyclopedias, and periodicals. Typically, research in the library will involve determining the exact subject of the research and looking up the key words in a legal encyclopedia, digest, or treatise. In these volumes may be found references to statutes and cases, which may then be located in the appropriate volumes.

One major difficulty in using books for legal research is framing the appropriate subject or issue. Sometimes the researcher will use one word and the digest will use another. In that case, he or she must look the word up in the digest's index. This process can be time consuming, particularly in those situations where the proper word cannot readily be found.

Once the appropriate cases and statutes are found, their citations must be checked to confirm that they are the most current cases on that subject and to be certain they have not been changed or overruled. Checking citations manually is often slow and tedious since several volumes of citations may have to be investigated to be sure all subsequent time periods are found. In general, the researcher may spend more time trying to find the proper material than reading the relevant cases and statutes.

Law libraries are expensive to maintain. Subscriptions to update services must be kept, and someone must insert the updates when they are received. Although cases are published in volumes chronologically, most other series distribute pocket parts that include updated information and are inserted in the back of the current volume. Sometimes it takes several months before the information is received and inserted; thus, in many situations, book research may not be current.

Some law offices maintain law libraries with a minimum number of books, such as state cases and statutes. If the researcher must conduct research in other volumes, a public law library must be utilized. This necessitates the researcher traveling to the library to complete the research during library hours. Although attorneys and paralegals often conduct their research in the late evening or early morning hours, most law libraries are not open during those hours. Even if the researcher is able to be at the library during its operating hours, the required volume may not be available because it is in use by another researcher. A considerable amount of time may be wasted just looking for a specific volume among those being used by researchers in the library.

There are, however, many instances where library research is beneficial. Some small law offices cannot afford subscriptions to the computerized research services or, if they can, may prefer to conduct preliminary research in the books before signing on to the service.

Many law firms use a combination of manual and computerized legal research to cut down on expenses and to be sure their results are timely. Even sole practitioners may share the expenses of computerized services with their colleagues in a shared-library arrangement. That is, the lawyers may share office space but have their own practices. This allows them to share the benefits and the costs of a law library as well.

A comprehensive study of manual legal research is beyond the scope of this textbook. The material provided is merely a comparison of the advantages and disadvantages of manual and computerized legal research.

ONLINE LEGAL DATABASES

Subscription services are available to Westlaw and LEXIS online. Costs vary by the number of databases the subscriber wishes to access and by whether the subscriber has a monthly payment contract with unlimited use or based on an hourly fee. Both of these subscription systems are available on the Internet. The user may access the appropriate Web page, then key in a user name and password to enter the service. More information about these services may be obtained at the following Web addresses:

http://www.westlaw.com

http://www.lexis.com

LOISLAW®

On-line research may be conducted at Loislaw at a relatively low cost. It provides Internet- and CD-ROM-based libraries with access to more than ten million pages of state and federal sources. Paralegal programs that are approved by the American Bar Association may obtain free subscriptions to the Loislaw® system for teaching purposes. Its Web page is located at:

http://www.loislaw.com

SUMMARY

This chapter gives a summary of the different types of computer-assisted research that are available. Basic terms are defined in the glossary. A majority of students will already be familiar with how a computer operates. Some may also have performed some basic research using the Internet. Therefore, a synopsis of the basics is provided here. Chapter 2 provides a brief description of the volumes available for manual research and the advantages and disadvantages of each.

REVIEW QUESTIONS

1. Define CALR. What is included in this system?
2. What are the advantages of performing initial research manually?
3. What is e-mail? Describe its advantages over regular mail.
4. What is entailed in manual research? How is manual research performed?
5. What are the advantages of computerized legal research over manual research?

PRACTICAL PROBLEMS

1. You are employed as a paralegal in the law firm of Jeffries and Daniels, which performs all of its research manually. Mr. William M. Jeffries has asked you to prepare a memorandum outlining the major reasons why your firm should subscribe to one of the on-line research services, such as Westlaw or LEXIS. After researching the various computerized research systems, prepare a memorandum to Mr. Jeffries outlining the

reasons your firm should subscribe to the service and recommending one service in particular.

2. Group Project: Conduct a survey of the law firms in your community to determine what percentage of them use computerized legal research.

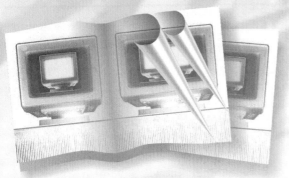

CHAPTER **2**

Manual Research

INTRODUCTION

Manual research requires the use of a library of books to accomplish research tasks. As discussed in Chapter 1, it may be more time consuming and less timely than computerized research. However, the following are certain situations where it is advantageous:

- Small law firms may not be able to afford expensive subscription services.
- The overabundance of material available via electronic research can be overwhelming for the researcher who is more familiar with manual research.
- You may find that research material on the Internet is not organized as neatly and concisely as in books.
- The reliability of research obtained from the Internet is frequently questionable.

You can do manual research and be able to ascertain the reliability of the author and publisher of the material. However, some computerized legal research materials may not be from dependable sources or you may not be able to find it the next time you look. Web pages are constantly changing, and the site you used for research yesterday may have moved tomorrow. With ever-changing Web pages, the credibility of the research sources on these pages becomes an issue of concern.

Law books have remained durable and permanent. Simply pick up a book; it is not the same as accessing an electronic source. Hyperlinks that are sent in an e-mail change and have to be constantly updated by the researcher, whereas the books are easily updated by the publisher merely by the use of pocket parts.

Research viewed on a computer screen is limited to the size of the monitor. However, as any manual researcher knows, several books may be spread open on a desk at the same time enabling you to switch from one to another while conducting research on a given topic.

PRIMARY SOURCES

Many traditional researchers begin their search in the primary sources of cases and statutes. State and federal statutes are categorized into codes that may be annotated. Within the annotations the researcher may find extensive information on related cases or other statutes, as well as references to law review articles and treatises.

Digests enable the researcher to find information about cases in various subject areas. Brief synopses of the facts of the case are provided so that you may locate appropriate related cases. However, these cases relate to the specific topic only. Cases dealing with important collateral issues may not be readily found using the digests.

Once a particular topic is found in the digest, you must read through the brief paragraphs on the cases to determine whether or not a case is applicable to the research topic at hand. Often these synopses are very short and omit some of the issues in the actual case. Or they may seem to be directly related to the issue, but are not pertinent when the researcher finds the actual case. Therefore, each case found in the digest that appears to be related to the issue must be found and analyzed. Sometimes further authority must also be found. This method may be overly time consuming and yield few beneficial results.

Although books may be helpful for searching outlines, tables of contents, and indices, the actual reading of all cases, codes, and annotations that appear to be related to the issue may be a waste of time if the necessary information is not found. You may be so focused on one narrow issue that you miss important collateral areas that could strengthen your case.

SECONDARY SOURCES

Using secondary sources as a starting point for research may assist the researcher by providing help from legal experts to analyze concepts and cases, and to prepare documents. Timely information can be found in treatises and law review articles devoted to specific areas of legal expertise. If the issue being researched is current and timely, there may be law review articles written on the subject by recognized legal scholars. These scholarly works provide assistance in specific subject areas.

Legal Dictionaries and Thesauruses

In some cases, the researcher may not be familiar with a legal term being used. A legal dictionary is useful for finding the definition. In some cases, the legal meaning is different from the everyday meaning of a word. The legal thesaurus is useful in finding synonyms for a word; this is a particularly valuable tool when writing a legal memorandum or brief.

Legal Encyclopedia

Legal encyclopedias are useful in doing preliminary research on general legal topics. Universally accepted legal principles are presented in standard language that is usually easy to understand. Obtaining this general knowledge of the law on a given topic may assist the researcher in finding more specific information. Be sure to use the pocket parts for the most recent information about a given topic.

Law Review Articles

A major advantage of searching law review articles is their accuracy. The articles are checked for accuracy by a team of law students who are members of the *Law Review* at that particular law school. All citations are examined for timeliness and correctness. The material also guides the researcher to appropriate primary sources.

Treatises and Practice Guides

Treatises are usually limited in scope and deal only with the particular subject at hand. Related issues in other areas of the law may not be included.

Practice guides may be *very* limited in scope. Limited authority is provided for the laws discussed therein. For example, you may find that a particular issue has a citation for only the statute or possibly a leading case that is relevant to that issue.

COMBINATION RESEARCH

The experienced researcher uses a combination of primary and secondary materials, depending on the type of research being conducted. When a complete issue is being examined for purposes of a research memorandum, both primary and secondary sources are beneficial. Preliminary questions must be asked to determine whether the authority is relevant in the particular jurisdiction, whether it is mandatory or persuasive, and whether it is current. In many cases, the researcher will have to perform preliminary research as preparation for locating the material being sought.

In some cases, finding relevant information is restricted by the researcher's own vocabulary. Using the wrong term for a relevant term may yield erroneous results. You should always be willing to consider the need to search for additional terms to yield the proper results. Keeping a thesaurus at hand and listing similar terms may prevent costly errors.

Framing the issue is critical; the researcher must focus on the points of law that need to be discussed. If the issue is not written correctly, a considerable amount of time may be spent researching collateral issues that are not relevant to the case at hand.

Listed below are some steps to consider when doing manual research:

1. Know exactly what you are looking for.

   The paralegal or other law office assistant conducting the research should be clear as to the focus of the research and the expectations of the attorney who gave the assignment. For instance, you may be called upon to do a complete research memorandum, or you may be asked to update the cases in a legal brief.

2. Frame an issue statement.

   Before answering a question, the researcher must first determine the question itself. An improperly formed issue statement may lead to useless research. Therefore, be as specific as possible when framing an issue. Do not be content with an issue like, "Was the defendant negligent?". Delve into the situation to determine the specifics of the case. It is usually easier to broaden a narrow issue statement than to scale down the research when the issue is too broad. A considerable amount of time and money may be wasted in perusing irrelevant material. Once a narrow issue statement has been identified, the researcher should use the thesaurus to find like terms to use for a proper search.

3. Determine whether to start with primary or secondary authority.

    See the sections above that are related to manual research in primary and secondary authorities. In general, if your case involves violation of a statute, you would start by finding the statute along with its annotations. If your case relates to a broader area, or one with which you are not familiar, then it may be better to start with secondary authority to enable you to learn more about that particular legal specialty. Be sure to use sources in your own jurisdiction: sources for your state for a state case, or federal sources for your state for a federal case.

4. Find appropriate authority for your case.

    Once the issue statement has been framed, the researcher should begin to find the appropriate authority for that issue. Whether you start with primary or secondary authority is often dependent on the extent of the research project and the nature of the case itself.

    Ask yourself the following questions before beginning:

    a. Which court is this case in?

    b. Is the case governed by a state or federal statute?

    c. Is there likely to be case authority in the appropriate jurisdiction?

    d. Is the subject of the case familiar or should I do preliminary research in a secondary source?

5. Expand the issue statement.

    If you have framed a narrow issue statement under step 2, read that issue carefully. Decide what other words with the same meaning may be used. Use relevant terminology in determining additional key words. Be sure that your expansion of terms is done with specificity. The more specific the key words are, the more likely you are to avoid wasting time in finding irrelevant material. Decide if there are any relevant subissues that will have a bearing on your research, and develop key words for these subissues.

6. Conduct your research.

Make a list of the sources you wish to use in answering your issue question. Systematically go through all of these materials to be sure you are using the most recent material. Use pocket parts for statutes and secondary sources and the latest opinions for case research. Remember to Shepardize your sources.

7. Assemble and analyze your response.

One of the most difficult parts of a research query is determining exactly which of the authorities are relevant to the case at hand. You must determine which authorities will be used to answer your issue statement.

In some cases, an inexperienced researcher may spend many hours finding irrelevant information before an applicable authority is discovered. It is tempting to include these items in your research memorandum so that your employer/attorney is aware of the effort spent finding it. However, only relevant information should be included. If opposing authority beneficial to the adverse party's case is found, include this in your research memorandum.

Read all authority and ascertain the reasoning of the court in reaching its conclusions. This argument may often be used by the attorney to convince the court to rule for your client by following the prior court's reasoning. On the other hand, comprehensive legal analysis of the facts and the law may distinguish the prior case from your case by proposing a different ruling by this court.

In preparing your research memorandum, prioritize the authorities that have been analyzed by their value to your case. Figure 2-1 shows a list of priorities to be used when assigning value to your authorities. The list is in the order of relevance to the court. It is important to remember that the only time a case decision will take precedence over a statute is if the statute is found to violate the Constitution.

UPDATING YOUR RESEARCH

All authorities selected for your research must be authenticated by looking them up in the citators to determine whether or not they have been overruled. When performing this step in your manual research, several

FEDERAL CASES

1. The United States Constitution

2. Opinions of the United States Supreme Court

3. Federal statutes and administrative regulations

4. Court of Appeals decisions of the federal court having jurisdiction over your case

5. Court of Appeals decisions of federal courts outside the jurisdiction in number 4

6. Opinions of the Federal District Court in your case's jurisdiction

7. Opinions of the Federal District Court outside your case's jurisdiction

STATE CASES

1. The United States Constitution

2. Opinions of the United States Supreme Court

3. Statutes (codes) and administrative regulations of the state having jurisdiction

4. Opinions of the State Supreme Court having jurisdiction

5. Opinions of the State Appellate Court having jurisdiction

6. Opinions of other State Appellate Courts within the state

FIGURE 2-1 Authorities' Priorities

volumes must be found that cover the relevant time periods. For example, suppose you are updating a case that was decided in 1995 that you wish to use as authority. Look this case up in all citators from 1995 to the present time. This may involve finding a bound volume of the citator as well as several paperback volumes. Make a list of the time periods covered in each separate volume so that you can check the list upon completion to be sure no time periods were left out. Figures 2-2 and 2-3 on page 15 show the steps to follow in updating cases and statutes using a citator service.

If you have a subscription to a computerized research system, the updating is much quicker. There are codes that can be keyed into the computer and used for updating after you type in the citation for the case or statute. While manual research updating may take several hours, the same process may be completed on the computer in minutes. One research system quotes a ten-second updating time per case or statute.

---

1. Find the exact citation for the case being updated, including volume, series, and page number of the first page of the case.

2. Find the appropriate citator for that particular series of cases, such as the *California Reporter*. The name of the series will appear on the cover of the citator.

3. Find the hardbound citator that covers the volume number of the case you are updating within that series of publications.

4. Find the page for the case you are updating. Note that the series and volume will appear on the top of each page. The volume number will also appear in large bold letters on the page itself. Look down the list of page numbers within the appropriate volume until yours is located.

5. All case citations listed under your case represent cases that cited the instant case. To the left of the citation are codes that may be found in the front of the citator. Be sure to be especially watchful for the "o" code, which means that particular case overruled your case, or the "r" code, which means the decision was reversed. Superscripts within the citation itself refer to the headnote numbers from the case being "Shepardized."

6. Once you have updated the case using the bound volume, go through the same process for all paperbound volumes published subsequent thereto. When you are finished, check to be sure that all dates after the date of your case have been found.

FIGURE 2-2 Updating Cases Using Citators ("Shepardizing")

1. Find the exact citation for the statute, including the number of the statute, the number or name of the topic, and the name and year of the publication in which it appeared. For example, you may wish to update California Penal Code Section 211.2 from 1995. Some states separate their statutes into codes; others merely use a numbering system for the statute itself.

2. Find the hardbound volume of the citator that covers the particular series of statutes you are seeking, as well as for the years 1995 and beyond. This information will appear on the cover of the citator.

3. Use the same system used in steps 1 and 2 when updating cases. That is, search through the citator itself until you find the topic of your statute and the page number. Verify that all statutes appearing below the citation for the initial statute cited your statute.

4. Codes for the statutes are different from the cases and may be found in the front of the citator volume. The equivalent of the "o" for overruled in cases is "r" for repealed or "a" for amended in statutes.

5. Just as you did when updating cases, look in each subsequent paperback volume of the citator until all dates after your statute have been found.

FIGURE 2-3 Updating Statutes Using Citators

SUMMARY

This chapter provides a brief summary of the manner in which manual research is conducted. Most paralegal programs require the student to complete an extensive course in this type of research. Therefore, for those students who have not had the standard legal research course, the chapter provides a brief background into the methods used. The material will serve as a review for those students who have already completed the course.

Primary and secondary sources are distinguished. A brief description is given of each type of authority. A list of steps to consider is provided for preparation of research projects.

REVIEW QUESTIONS

1. What are the advantages of using the library books for a research project?
2. Describe the reliability of Internet research.
3. Under what circumstances would the researcher use secondary sources as a starting point?
4. When would you use a legal encyclopedia for research?
5. Why would you use law review articles for a research project?

PRACTICAL PROBLEMS

1. Find a state supreme court case in your state that is five years old and deals with drunk driving laws. Shepardize that case to determine whether it has been overruled or changed. Give the case citation, a brief description of the facts, and indicate whether the case is still valid. Give the Shepard's volume and page number of the location of the case.
2. Find your state's statute that deals with burglary of a residence. Update the statute using Shepard's. Give the statute number, a brief description, and note whether it has been changed. Indicate the Shepard's volume and page number of the statute's update location.

CHAPTER 3

Introduction to Internet Research

INTRODUCTION

The Internet has become by far the fastest growing source for legal research. A vast amount of material has been placed on Web pages for federal and state research. Although a considerable amount of material is available on the Internet, care must be taken to be sure that the Web sites used provide pertinent and timely information. The official sources for legal information provide the best foundation for finding research material that has been validated. Remember, anyone may establish a Web page; it is up to the reader to determine its value and authenticity.

The Internet provides the opportunity for the researcher to find many sources in addition to those used in legal research. Sources for factual research are common on the Internet. E-mail provides the opportunity to communicate with others who may be helpful in finding pertinent information. Search engines enable the researcher to use key words to find information. Specific Web pages with which the researcher is already familiar may provide further sources of material.

CONNECTING TO THE INTERNET

In order to connect to the Internet, you will need a modem on your computer as well as a subscription with an Internet provider. If you are connecting from your school or business, the computer you are using must have *Internet access,* that is, the ability to connect to the Internet.

A modem allows computers to talk to each other via telephone lines. If your computer has a modem, it will also have a cord with plugs that must be connected to your computer as well as to a telephone wall socket. If you have one telephone line, when you are using the modem, no telephone calls may be made or received. Many people who use the Internet frequently will have two separate telephone lines, one for the telephone and one for the modem. In this way, you may still receive and make telephone calls while you are using the modem. However, you will then have a double telephone bill.

There are many providers through which you can purchase Internet access. Investigate different companies. Talk to your friends who use the Internet to determine which providers they use and if they are happy with their services. Some providers have frequent disconnects, which can be frustrating when you are in the middle of a research project and are suddenly disconnected from the line. If you are connected from work or school, this decision will have been made by the individuals in charge at that location. However, it is usually recommended that you have access from your home computer as well.

NAMES AND ADDRESSES ON THE INTERNET————

At your office or school, you may have an Internet name and address already assigned to you. For instance, at the school where the author taught, all employees use their first initial and last name for a name and the school's Internet address for an address. Thus, my address would be:

JLong@rh.cc.ca.us

After the person's name use an @ sign prior to writing the address.

If you have Internet access at home, you will have to choose a name and the provider will generally have its own address. For instance, if you were using America Online, your address would be:

_____@aol.com

Many Internet experts advise individuals not to use their first names in their screen name. Therefore, a typical screen name using the above address might be JLong. The name and address then become:

JLong@aol.com

This is the style of a name and address someone might use when sending you e-mail, discussed below.

E-MAIL

Sending correspondence via the Internet is practically instantaneous. You may write to someone in another part of the country or world, or perhaps across town, and the e-mail will be received within minutes of the time you sent it. Internet providers have forms to use to send e-mail. In the name portion, use the name as discussed above with the appropriate address, similar to the manner in which you send regular mail (known as "snail mail" on the Internet). If you dislike typing, voice recognition software programs are available whereby you can talk into a microphone and the computer does the typing for you, similar to using dictating equipment.

Internet names may also give you information about the location of an individual. For instance, the following sites or locations are indicated by the extensions in their names:

.com   commercial site (often used by private Internet providers)
.gov   a government site
.mil   a military site
.org   an organization
.edu   education
.ca   California or Canada
.uk   United Kingdom

NAMES FORMAT FOR E-MAIL

Most Internet e-mail addresses are comprised of capital and lowercase letters. A lowercase letter is usually appropriate in any case. No spaces should be placed in an Internet e-mail name. When giving your name to someone, spell out each portion of the name unless the spelling is obvious. "@" should be given as "at."

WEB PAGE ADDRESSES

In addition to the names used for e-mail, other names are used to reach the various Web pages. These addresses are known as location numbers or URLs (Uniform Resource Locator). In order to access a page on the

Internet, the URL must be used. If you wished to access the Web page for West Publishing Company, you would type the following address in the "Go to" section of your Internet provider after you have accessed your account:

http://www.westpub.com

This address is the URL for West Publishing Company. Most large corporations have their own Web pages, which are accessed via their Web address (or URL).

Note that Internet addresses generally begin with "http://www." and in many cases are followed by an abbreviation of the company's name you are accessing. For instance, the Web site for Northwest Airlines is "http://www.nwa.com". When you key in the address at the "go to" portion of your screen, you will be taken to the Web page for Northwest Airlines. This information is useful if you are doing a search to find a particular organization and are unable to find it. Sometimes just abbreviating the name and using ".com" will take you to the site.

SEARCHES

Several search tools are available to help you to find information on the Internet. Your Internet provider will usually have its own search engine, or you may prefer to use others as well. Some of the more common are menu driven. That is, they provide a list of categories from which you can search. Examples are YAHOO, GOPHER, and VERONICA.

Others provide a key word search that enables you to list all key words in which you are interested. An example is AOLNET located at:

http://www.aol.com

The computer will search the Internet and provide you with an abstract of all documents that have your key words within them. They are listed by percentage of occurrence, with the highest numbers first. Suppose you want articles that give you information on New York cases involving grounds for divorce. You would key the following words into the search box:

New York Divorce Grounds

If you want the exact wording to appear in the documents, then type the key words in quotes as follows:

"New York grounds for divorce"

Sometimes the key words will have to be changed or modified to yield a more specific search result. At other times the key words may be too specific and you may have to make them more general. Be prepared for a lengthy search no matter what the subject is, as there is a vast amount of information out there on the Internet.

SEARCH ENGINES

Yahoo represents one of the most extensive collections of links to Web sites on the Internet. It contains a tremendous collection of links to law firms with Web pages. Approximately 30,000 Web locations may be found by a search on Yahoo, which is located at:

http://www.yahoo.com

Some Internet providers allow access to Yahoo by merely keying "Yahoo" in the "Go to" category.

Most searches may be conducted in the same manner. Type in your key word(s) on the search page; in a few seconds the results will follow.

Internet Card Catalog

This site works much like a standard library card catalog. It is an excellent subject matter index for most sources available on the Internet. For general or factual research, this may be the best starting point available. It may be accessed at:

**http://www.info.cern.ch/hypertext/DataSources/bySubject/
Overview.html**

HYPERTEXT LINKS

Sometimes when you are reading information on a Web page, you will notice text that is underlined or shown in a different color. This text represents a hypertext link, called a "hyperlink," to another Web page. If you click your mouse on that word or group of words, it will take you immediately to another area of the Web. In some cases, you will find Web pages with lists of hypertext links in a given subject area. For instance, some colleges provide hyperlinks on their Web pages to different areas of the college or to research materials about given topics.

For example, suppose you were on the Web page for the Codes of California. Listed there will be the various codes, all names underlined as hypertext links. If you click on the **Penal Code**, you will be immediately taken to the Penal Code of California. Once you find a page to which you may wish to refer in the future, you may bookmark that page to enable you to have immediate access to it. Some systems refer to this bookmark as "favorite places." After you bookmark a page, you can click on its title from the bookmark list and immediately go to that page without taking the time to do a search or key in its address.

GRAPHICS IN BROWSERS

GUIs (Graphical User Interfaces) are used in browser programs such as Explorer, Netscape, and Mosaic, and are displayed as icons or graphics on the Web pages that enable you to execute commands on your computer. For example, icons may be available for stopping, going back to the previous page, going to the home page, scrolling, or going forward. Some of the commands on these pages are similar to those used in Windows. Browser programs that use icons or graphics for these purposes are much easier to navigate.

GETTING STARTED

The steps for using the Internet for research purposes are given below. The information superhighway is merely a few mouse clicks away.

1. Open Your Browser

Be sure your computer is turned on and look for the icon that shows your particular browser. Double click on that icon with your mouse. Depending on where you are signing on from, you will probably need your user name and password to get "online." Additionally, your school may have a special Web page that acts as the home page when you first go online from your college. Generally, the browser takes a few minutes to load, so be patient. When the hourglass shows on the computer screen, your browser is loading. It is fully loaded when the hourglass turns into an arrow.

Think of the home page as your home on the Internet. From your "home" you may visit many other sites, but returning home just takes a click on the "home" icon.

2. Find Other Sites

Scroll down your home page to become familiar with its contents. If you see an item of interest and it is underlined or in color, click on it to be taken to its site. (Note that this is known as a "hyperlink.") You may continue to click on hyperlinks on subsequent pages several times and may even find yourself in another part of the world. Now look at your watch to see the amount of time that has elapsed. Time passes quickly on the Internet.

3. Go Back Home

Returning to your home page may be done quickly or with detours along the way. Suppose you want to return to your home page immediately. Click on the "Home" icon and you are home again.

But what if you previously found an interesting site and forgot how to get to it? Just click on the "back" button and it will move you backward to the other sites you have been on. Click "home" to go home by driving forward and directly; click "back" to go home by driving backward with stops along the way.

Another method for retracing your steps is by using the "View History" command from the pull-down menu. The names of all previously visited pages since leaving "home" will appear. Click on the one that you want to revisit.

DISPLAYING ADDRESS OF CURRENT LOCATION

Browsers usually display the address of the present location in a box at the top of the screen. In many cases, showing the location is provided as a default setting; however, in those cases where the default has to be set, follow these steps:

1. Select "Show Location" or "Show Current URL" from the Options pull-down menu.
2. Follow the instructions for turning that option on.
3. Check the address portion at the top of the page to be sure the current address is displayed.
4. If possible, change the Options to reflect this as the default option.

INFORMATION ABOUT THE INTERNET

The best information about the Internet may be found on the Internet itself. Do a key word search using the word "Internet," and many items will be displayed. Click on those that actually give you information about the Internet. Check the date on the home page to determine the last date it was updated. Most home pages will display this date. If the update was recent, then the home page information is probably up to date.

But suppose the page was not updated in the last year. That means that all information on the page was probably current a year ago. With the vast number of changes occurring every day on the Internet, you would not want to use this page for current information.

OBSOLETE URLs

Sometimes you will click into a page from your bookmarks and find that the page no longer exists. In that case, you may have to do a new search for its location. Many pages change locations often, and the page you found three months ago may not be there today. Sometimes the new page address is given on the old page; other times you may have to do a completely new search to find it. In this case, be sure to delete the obsolete page from your bookmarks and add the new page name.

TIMING OUT

Some Internet pages are very popular and are difficult to access because of the number of individuals trying to access them at the same time. In those cases, you may get a "timed out" message when attempting to reach the site. This is similar to a busy signal on a telephone. Keep trying until you reach the site. In some cases, if a page is taking a long time to load, it helps to hit "stop" and "reload" to reload the page more quickly.

ETIQUETTE ON THE INTERNET ("NETIQUETTE")

Just as in everyday life, there are certain things that you should do and others that you should not do on the Internet. The key to remember is to be polite, whether it be in an e-mail message, a bulletin board posting, or a chat room meeting. Remember that the individuals with whom you are communicating cannot see your facial expressions and do not know whether you are smiling or frowning.

Some individuals who subscribe to newsgroups intentionally try to offend others and are entertained when another person becomes offended. These people post on newsgroups and oppose the consensus of the group in a derogatory fashion. For instance, one may post to a newsgroup on golf and say "Golf is a dumb game. How could anyone chase a little ball around a golf course?" Of course, the golfers who post to the group are offended and wish to respond. This person welcomes the responses and is happy to get the group riled up. The common Internet name for this individual is a "SNERT." These antagonists are looking for a reaction and their messages are known as "flame bait."

The term used in these situations is "flame," which means a communication that vehemently disapproves of someone else's posting. It is much better to be polite in your postings than to have to be "flamed." If you are the source of offense to someone, even if innocently, it is best to apologize.

Beware of using all capital letters in your postings; this is known as "shouting" on the Internet. It may be used occasionally for emphasis but is usually frowned upon.

When responding to a message, it may be appropriate to quote part of the previous message, but never copy the whole message. Make your messages brief and to the point.

Separate paragraphs with one blank line, just as you do in regular correspondence. Do not make your e-mails all one paragraph if several topics are discussed.

Proofread your messages to be certain that spelling and sentence structure are correct. Proofread them a second time to be sure they will not offend the recipient. If you are attempting to inject humor into the message, then use the emoticon for a happy face:

:))) or :-)))

Answering E-mail

E-mail should be answered within a day or two of the time it is received. Individuals who use e-mail for their correspondence expect prompt responses. Think of e-mail as you think of a telephone call. Write return e-mails as promptly as you would return a phone message.

SECURITY ON THE INTERNET

Much has been written about security problems on the Internet. How can you be assured that when you send an e-mail it will be received and read by only the recipient? What about those situations when one person gets all of the e-mail for a large department and distributes it in printed form? Are there hackers out there who can get into anyone's e-mail? Unfortunately, there are serious security problems in the use of the Internet. Service providers have the capability to access subscribers' e-mail. The same is true for system administrators for large organizations. However, the Internet is probably just as secure as most other communication devices.

With the advent of cordless and cellular telephones, individual conversations are readily available to anyone with the proper interception equipment. Scramblers are available for most devices, but both parties must have the same type of scrambler for the message to be received and transmitted properly and securely. The same is true for the Internet. There are devices on the market to encode e-mail, but the sender needs an encoder device and the receiver needs a decoder device.

An equally prevalent problem is sending the e-mail to the wrong person. Most Internet providers enable you to have your own address book of e-mail addresses for people to whom you frequently send e-mail. The list is accessible by a click of the mouse; the address is put into the e-mail with a click of the mouse; the e-mail is sent with a click of the mouse. In three clicks you can access the address book, select the address, and send an e-mail. Suppose in your haste you click on the wrong address. Instantly that e-mail is sent to the wrong person.

Imagine the scenario of you keying in someone's name and e-mail address. One typographical error might send that e-mail to the wrong person. Anyone with an e-mail account knows how easy it is to receive an e-mail intended for someone else.

Confidential communications should not be sent via e-mail unless a coding or encryption system is operative. It may be beneficial for the sender and recipient to have one of these systems whereby messages can be encoded by the software and decoded upon receipt by the recipient.

PASSWORD SECURITY

Many people think their communication is secure because they access their Internet account via a password. This may be the case if an uncommon password is used. However, most people use common words, names, or numbers. Password thieves know the most common names to try to access another's account. Try to make your password something only you know. Do not use your social security number, your address, your age, your date of birth, or any names in your family. Memorize your password and do not write it down where anyone else might find it.

It has been said that anyone going through an office complex late at night would be able to find a majority of the passwords by just looking at people's computers. Some individuals use a post-it note attached to their computer screen with their password written on it. Any note found with a one-word name written on it is likely a password.

LISTSERVS

A listserv is similar to a subscription to e-mail on a given topic. Once you register for the listserv, all mail sent out to the listserv is also sent to you. It is a free service that may prove valuable for individuals interested in various topics. For instance, the author subscribes to a listserv of paralegal educators and receives daily communications about information of interest in that area.

There are two different types of listservs, one which enables everyone on the list to post messages (discussion lists) and one which only allows certain individuals to post (distribution list). In order to subscribe to a listserv, you must use the address for the listserv. Once you have subscribed to the listserv, you may use the address for the discussion group in order to post to the group. Or you can key a response to an e-mail that has been sent by the listserv to you and hit "reply to all."

Once you have subscribed to a listserv, you will receive a confirmation back via e-mail almost immediately. Usually you will be required to send a confirmation that you in fact have subscribed to the listserv. The next e-mail you receive from the listserv will list detailed instructions on the protocol for the group. It is a good idea to print this message so that you know the proper procedures for this particular group.

The best way to find a listserv of interest is by word of mouth. Books are also available with names of listservs. Once you subscribe to one listserv, you will often receive information about others as well. Suppose, however, that after subscribing to one listserv, you are interested in finding out what others are available in that topic. You may send an e-mail to the listserv address with the following information in the body:

LISTS GLOBAL/law

LISTS GLOBAL/education

or any other topic in which you are interested after the "/" symbol.

NEWSGROUPS (USENET)

Newsgroups provide an international bulletin board with thousands of topics and hundreds of thousands of different conversations. There are newsgroups on every topic imaginable from academic discussions to sporting events. Within newsgroups you can find images, sounds, and software that you can download to your computer. Newsgroups provide the second widest usage of the Internet; they are second only to e-mail.

A newsreader program is required for anyone who wishes to participate in a newsgroup. This allows the user to subscribe to newsgroups so that you can read newsgroup articles as well as post your own messages. Major categories include computers, news, recreation, sports, and various special, regional, or local groups. Often a group will be created that relates to a current, high-profile news event, such as the plight of Afghanistan.

Newsgroups allow an individual to post notices, send or distribute notices to the group, and publish discussion items. You may think of these newsgroups as giant bulletin boards or discussion groups.

SUMMARY

The basics of accessing the Internet and the method for conducting a simple search are described in this chapter. Search methods are described, and sample problems discussed. The steps for conducting research on the Internet are given, along with some Internet protocol.

REVIEW QUESTIONS

1. Does your college have a Web page? If so, what is its address?
2. List three items of interest on your college's Web page.
3. What is the difference between a listserv and a newsgroup?
4. What equipment is required in order to connect to the Internet?
5. How is a commercial site indicated in an Internet name?

PRACTICAL PROBLEMS

1. Suppose you would like to take a class at your college through the Internet. Find classes that you need to graduate in your major (including general education classes) that are offered online. How many units can you take by this method?

2. Locate the Web page of a major airline that flies from a city near you to Phoenix, Arizona. Find the round-trip fares for a flight leaving fourteen days from today and returning twenty-eight days from today. What is the URL address of the airline, the fare, and the flight information including date, time, and flight number? Do not actually make the reservation, but merely make an inquiry.

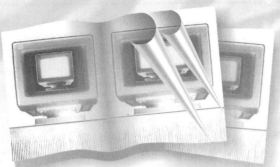

General Uses of the Internet

INTRODUCTION

In this chapter, we will explore the various tools available on the Internet and how to use them. We will discuss methods of communication, arrange travel, find individuals or businesses, and learn about traffic in your city.

E-MAIL

Even those individuals who do not do research on the Internet will use electronic mail, commonly known as e-mail. This represents a superior method of communicating whereby recipients are able to receive your messages almost immediately after you sent them. They may communicate back to you in the same fashion. The only necessary component is that both parties have an Internet address.

In today's business world, most offices are connected via e-mail. If the business has a LAN or a WAN, a connection to the Internet, or an online service, it will have e-mail capability. You may have noticed that most individuals with business cards now display their e-mail address on them. It is much more convenient to send someone an e-mail rather than to leave several messages on an answering machine. You may also send the same e-mail to several people at the same time, which adds to its efficiency. The greatest single activity used on the Internet is e-mail.

Imagine the tons of paper that are saved by the use of e-mail instead of standard "snail mail" sent through the postal service. From an environmental standpoint, envision how many trees are saved by e-mail.

E-mail has all of the advantages and none of the disadvantages of postal mail and telephone calls. It eliminates "phone tag" because it doesn't matter if the recipient is not at home when the e-mail is sent. It is much faster than the mails so the recipient gets your mail immediately. It is also less expensive than any other means of communication in that it is virtually free except for the cost of the Internet service and telephone line. If you have local access in the city where you live, then even the telephone charges are free. Most localities have local access numbers so that you connect to the Internet via a local number and send your e-mails over those same lines. Hence, there will be no charge for the telephone call. This holds true for anyone in the country, and also the world, who has an e-mail address. You can send an e-mail message to a friend in London, for example, as long as he or she has an e-mail address, at no cost.

Each individual with e-mail has a unique mailing address. No two people may have the same address. In order to send an e-mail, you must know the person's exact address or your mail will either go to the wrong person or be returned to you marked "address unknown." Many Internet providers have an address book set up for you so that you can store other people's e-mail addresses in your own database. Many companies and schools have an online directory set up as an address book for you within your e-mail system.

But suppose you would like to have free e-mail and do not necessarily need Internet service. Some of the larger, well-established companies providing this service include the following:

1. Hotmail
   http://www.hotmail.com
2. iName
   http://www.iname.com
3. NetAddress
   http://www.netaddress.com

Free e-mail is also provided through major directory sites such as:

1. Yahoo
   http://www.yahoo.com

2. AltaVista
http://www.altavista.com

3. Excite
http://www.excite.com

One disadvantage of these free e-mail systems is that usually e-mail cannot be composed offline at your own pace, a service which is available through most Internet providers.

However, the major advantage of these systems is that one may send and receive messages from any computer with an Internet connection and a browser. Travelers may thus access e-mail from business centers, other offices, airline clubs, cyber cafes, and hotel computer kiosks, without the necessity of carrying a laptop and dealing with the special plugs and adapters that are often required in foreign countries, and without the fear of the laptop being lost or stolen.

America Online enables its users to access their e-mail from another computer by using the Web at:

http://www.aol.com/netmail/home.html

Therefore, if you are an AOL subscriber, traveling, and have access to another computer, you may gain access to your e-mail account by using the above Web address. During a recent cruise in Europe, the author was able to gain Internet access from the ship's computers and maintain contact with individuals via her AOL e-mail account.

PARTS OF THE E-MAIL

1. Caption or Heading

The caption of your e-mail message resembles that of an inter-office memorandum. It contains the following items:

TO:

SUBJECT:

The date you send the e-mail will appear automatically, as will your name. Often the time appears as well.

Be sure to key in the individual's exact e-mail address, along with the proper subject. In many cases, the Internet provider automatically places your e-mail address in the "FROM:" portion. If the recipient may not know the designation is your address, you may wish to put your name in the "SUBJECT:" portion of the caption. For instance, suppose your e-mail address is **Jdoe@ aol.com** and the recipient is not familiar with your last name. In the subject portion, you may put "From Jane Doe regarding Internet Meeting."

2. Copies

If you would like to send a copy of the e-mail to another individual, then key in the e-mail address here. If you would like to send a blind copy (one that the other recipients do not know is being sent), then put the person's address in parentheses as follows:

(Jdoe@aol.com)

Only Jdoe and you will know that he or she received a copy of the message.

3. Body

In the "message" portion of the e-mail, it is not necessary to use the same formal language often used in a letter. You should prepare the e-mail in block style, using a clear and concise writing style. If you want an answer within a certain time period, indicate the due date in the last paragraph of the e-mail, just as you would do in a letter. Although it is not possible to sign the e-mail, a closing with your name should be included.

4. Attachments

In some cases you may wish to attach other material to the e-mail. As long as you have this material on your computer in another file, you may do so. In order to send an attachment, you must key in the name of the document in the attachment box. Some providers enable you to search your files and drag a file into the e-mail.

You may attach documents, pictures, graphics, or any other item that you have on your computer's hard drive or on disk. You may wish to scan pictures and send them to a relative via e-mail. You may scan exhibits for a lawsuit and send them attached to an e-mail. You may wish to send a draft of a pleading or document for review by a colleague.

ORGANIZING YOUR E-MAIL

Most Internet providers furnish features that allow you to organize your e-mail into "In Boxes," "Out Boxes," "New Mail," "Sent Items," and other folders. Purge your "In Box" and "Sent Items" often to determine whether it is necessary to actually save each message. Your "In Box" will include all mail that has been sent to you and read by you, your "Out Box" will include all mail you have composed but not yet sent, your "New Mail" box will contain mail you have not yet read, and your "Sent Items" will include those e-mails you have sent out. Some Internet providers have additional e-mail designations.

Some Internet providers will only save your e-mail for a certain period of time to avoid taking up space on their system. Therefore, it may become necessary to make copies of the e-mail that you wish to save permanently. You may be able to save it to your hard drive or to a disk under another name.

SENDING YOUR E-MAIL

The best way to learn how to send e-mail is to actually do it. Open your e-mail program and we will go through the steps together. Let us begin by sending ourselves an e-mail message.

Key your e-mail address into the "To" section. Make your subject "Test" and type "test" in the message. Then click the "SEND" button, which is usually located to the right of the e-mail message. Instantly this message will be sent to you. Open the message, close it, and delete it. You may delete it by highlighting the message in the list of received messages. Be sure to close the message before highlighting it. Hit the "delete" key and the message will be deleted.

If you wish to delete several messages at the same time, highlight the first message you wish to delete. Holding down the "alt" and "shift" keys on the lower left of your keyboard, highlight the last message you wish to delete. Hit the "delete" key and all of those messages will be deleted.

ADDRESS BOOKS

Your Internet provider may furnish a place to put frequently used e-mail addresses, called an "address book." If available, it will have a place for the person or business name, designation, and e-mail address. To use the address book, open the "compose mail" or "write mail" icon and another icon will appear on the e-mail form called "Address Book." Click on the address book and a list of names will appear. Click on the name of the recipient of your e-mail and it will appear in the "To" portion of the e-mail. Different service providers have variations of this system.

You may wish to develop lists for different cases in your office. For example, under the general "Address Book" heading, you could make a general title called "Smith v. Jones," and list all e-mail addresses of individuals or entities that must be given notice of actions in that case.

CONDUCTING A SEARCH

Depending on the Internet provider utilized, various search engines are available on its home page to search the Internet for a given topic. For instance, suppose you want to find airlines Web pages. You would go to the search engine of the Internet provider and use the key word "airlines" for your search. If this provides too many pages, then you may wish to narrow your key words to produce a more specific group of page abstracts. The search engine provides a list of the Web pages that have your key words in their text, along with a brief description of each page. If you wish a certain set of words to appear in all responses, then your key words should be in quotation marks, such as "American Airlines." In this case, only those pages with the term "American Airlines" will show. Generally, the pages are listed in the order in which the largest number of key words appear with greatest frequency.

If the attorney or paralegal is traveling out of town and prefers a particular airline, a search using that airline's name would be conducted. Once the Web page for the airline is found, it can be "bookmarked" or added to "favorite places," depending on the Internet provider. By adding the Web address to this list, you may return to it by merely clicking its name on the list located under "bookmarks" or "favorite places." This method eliminates the need for conducting a search for the particular Web page each time you need it.

Various private Web pages exist for the purpose of providing search capabilities on many topics. One particularly comprehensive page that is very effective for doing general research is located at:

http://www.refdesk.com/

This site is useful if you cannot find a particular site by using your provider's search engine.

FINDING A PERSON OR BUSINESS ONLINE

Many Internet service providers have their own white pages to help you find people and yellow pages to find businesses. Searches may be conducted by name or geographical location. Suppose you have a friend in another state but do not know your friend's postal address. You could search by the person's name and the state to determine the address and, in many cases, telephone number. Note that some individuals and businesses are not included.

Several directories of lawyers exist online and will be discussed in the Legal Research section in chapter 5.

If you are looking for a telephone number, area code, or e-mail address, several Web databases are searched simultaneously by using this site:

http://www.555-1212.com

Yellow pages also exist for finding telephone numbers and addresses of businesses. Door-to-door driving directions may be obtained as well at:

http://www.zip2.com

Web pages exist of investigation firms that will search many databases, for a fee, to find people. One such site is located at:

http://www.ameri.com/sherlock/sherlock.htm

A good starting point for locating businesses, people, telephone numbers, e-mail addresses and to obtain maps is available at a site called "The Ultimates," located at:

http://www.theultimates.com

Many links to other Web sites are available at the above-noted site for searching white pages, yellow pages, e-mail addresses, and mapping services. Reverse residential telephone number searches may be performed as well. It is even possible to obtain the names of everyone who resides on a particular street along with their addresses and telephone numbers. If time is of the essence it may prove advantageous to hire an investigation firm rather than try to conduct the search alone.

The Social Security Administration provides a Web page to search over 60 million names to find death information. If you know the person's name and/or location, or social security number, a search may be conducted to determine the person's date of death and last known address. If you have only the person's name, all individuals with that name will be listed. The Web site is located at:

http://www.ssa.gov/SSA_Home.html

These search devices are useful if a party to an action is being sought for service purposes or if a search for an heir is being conducted.

MEETINGS ONLINE

Most of the publicity about "chat rooms" indicates that they are the places where dangerous things can happen because people often use other names and can remain relatively anonymous. However, the chat room may be effectively used for private meetings of businesses or law firms. Providers that have "chat" capability also provide the ability to set up a private chat room open by invitation only to specific individuals.

For instance, a marketing consultant in Canada may speak online to a client in New York without incurring long distance telephone charges by setting up a chat room for this purpose. A lawyer in Washington may set up a chat room meeting with members of the same firm located in New York. A judge at the World Court in New York may set up a room to meet with opposing lawyers from Japan and Russia to discuss a lawsuit regarding fishing rights. Staff meetings may be conducted with branch offices in other parts of the country or in other countries as well.

Endless possibilities exist for the constructive use of chat rooms to conduct business. Chat rooms are particularly valuable for dealing with individuals in other parts of the country, or the world, because long distance telephone charges are eliminated.

TRAVEL

Even with the use of chat rooms, it often becomes necessary to travel to other cities and countries. A considerable amount of information, including weather, hotels, cities, maps, and travel reservations, is available on the Internet.

Many travel agencies specialize in online reservations. Most airlines also have their own Web sites where reservations may be made. One interesting site that provides a considerable amount of travel information is located at:

http://www.thetrip.com

This site enables you to make plane reservations and provides guides for successful trips and travel news about different areas. It also has the ability to track a flight in progress once it leaves its point of origin. A new feature of this site is that it will notify up to three people by e-mail when a flight arrives at its destination. This may prove valuable in situations where people are arriving from different cities to attend a meeting.

Other sites that provide travel information and reservations include the following:

http://www.frommers.com

Travel information is provided by Arthur Frommer. The site is known as his Encyclopedia of Travel.

http://www.biztravel.com

This site specializes in business travel but also provides information for the leisure traveler. One may make flight, hotel, and car reservations, track frequent-flyer miles, and learn about special fares.

http://www.itn.com

The Internet Travel Network monitors the lowest fares between cities and provides flight reservations.

http://www.previewtravel.com

Preview Travel provides a means for making flight, hotel, and automobile reservations and reports on special fares when available. Their Farefinder searches airline databases to find the lowest fares between major United States cities.

In order to assist travelers who prefer to stay at hotels that have an in-room computer and Internet access, *Forbes* Magazine has developed "Rooms with a Clue" at:

http://www.forbes.com/tool/toolbox/clue/

The site provides information about rate and contact information and displays the hotel's telephone jack type, power plug type, and indicates whether the telephone system is digital or analog.

Travel Abroad

When traveling out of the country, you must have a passport. Information about obtaining passports is available on the State Department's home page at:

http://www.state.gov/index.html

The State Department provides a page where individuals may check a list of "travel warnings" to determine what countries are potentially dangerous for travelers. These warnings are issued when the State Department decides to recommend that Americans avoid travel to a particular country. Public announcements are provided that disseminate information about terrorist threats and other conditions posing significant risks to the security of American travelers. They are issued when there is a perceived threat and usually have Americans as a particular target group. Some examples of these announcements include short-term coups, bomb threats to airlines, violence by terrorists, and anniversary dates of specific terrorist events. This information is available at:

http://www.travel.state.gov/travel_warnings.html

General information about the large European cities may be found in a multimedia presentation of tours of these cities. The site includes films, photographs, audio, and virtual reality experiences. The site is available at:

http://www.iion.com/cineworld/index.html

Local Travel

Sometimes it is necessary to travel across town to an unknown location and you may need directions. Some sources for maps from one address to another are:

http://www.mapquest.com

http://www.mapblast.com

http://www.mapsonus.com

These sites provide directions and maps to all parts of the country. Figure 4-1 displays the main Mapquest search page.

Traffic Information

Traffic information for major cities throughout California is available on the Caltrans Web page, which may be found at:

http://www.dot.ca.gov

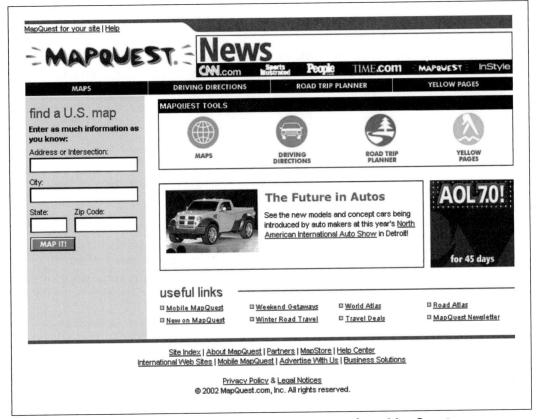

FIGURE 4-1 Mapquest Page. Reprinted with permission from **MapQuest.com**
© 2002 MapQuest.com.

This Web page began by providing California Department of Transportation information for freeways in the California metropolitan area. It now includes a larger cache of information, with such things as a listing of roadside rest areas throughout the state and details on the more scenic routes through California's rural areas.

Other information on the Caltrans Web page includes highway maps, real-time freeway maps detailing how fast traffic is moving in a given area, and information on accidents and road closures. Live traffic cameras are provided for the more problematic urban areas. The Los Angeles section is particularly comprehensive and indicates traffic patterns for all freeways in southern California.

Timeliness

Since Web pages may be created by anyone with the technical knowledge, it is imperative that each site being utilized be checked for timeliness and accuracy. Web pages usually have a date on the page itself. Find the source of the information on the page to determine whether this source is reliable. For instance, a travel advisory on the State Department's Web page would be more reliable than one offered by an unfamiliar individual on his or her Web page.

SUMMARY

A more detailed explanation of e-mail and its parts is discussed in this chapter. A general description of the methods of conducting a search is also provided. Various travel-related Internet sites are described, along with their value to the law office. For instance, the State Department Web site describes activities and problems in foreign countries to which the attorney may travel.

REVIEW QUESTIONS

1. List the sites that provide free e-mail.
2. What are the disadvantages of using one of the free e-mail systems?
3. What is included in the caption or heading of an e-mail?
4. How is a blind copy indicated on an e-mail?
5. List three sites that you may use when looking for a person in another city.

PRACTICAL PROBLEMS

1. The attorney for whom you work is traveling to the airport nearest your city for a meeting. Make a map from your office to the local airport.
2. The attorney is attending a business meeting in Jerusalem and has read in the newspaper that there may be unsafe travel conditions in that city.

Look on the State Department Web page to determine whether any travel advisories or cautions exist.

3. The attorney is attending a law convention at the Marriott Hotel in Indian Wells, California. Determine the least expensive air fare between your city and Palm Springs, California. Find a map to and from the Palm Springs airport and the hotel.

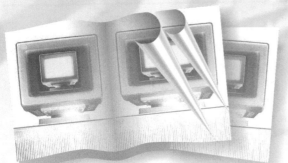

CHAPTER 5

Legal Research
on the Internet

INTRODUCTION

In the previous chapters you learned how to use the Internet and the World
Wide Web. A law office requires a considerable amount of this research.
For example, lawyers, paralegals, and other law office personnel send
e-mail to the firm, to other offices, and to other locations. They travel to
other parts of the country and world on business trips.

Finding adverse parties in lawsuits may be done via the various search
engines available on the Internet, as discussed in Chapter 3. Now we will
discuss the search mechanisms available to the legal profession, along with
the sites you would utilize for your legal research.

SEARCHES

The Library of Congress maintains a Web page that provides a catalog of
all available publications. You can search for any book that has been published and has an ISBN. Searches may be undertaken by title, key words,
or author. The site for the Library of Congress is located at:

http://lcweb.loc.gov/

One of the more comprehensive Web pages for finding information
about different areas of law is available at:

http://www.amicus.ca/links.html

This site provides information on specific practice areas along with background information on law-related topics. It is particularly useful for finding resources in a practice area with which you are unfamiliar or where more information is required than can be found under the federal or state links. This site includes the following practice areas:

1. Bankruptcy
2. Business law
3. Civil litigation
4. Commercial law
5. Constitutional law and civil rights
6. Corporate safety
7. Criminal law
8. Employment law
9. Family law
10. Health and disability law
11. Insurance law
12. Labor law
13. Environmental law
14. Probate law
15. Real property law
16. Personal injury

Links are provided on the laws of cyberspace as well as resources available on that topic. General links are provided to hardware and software information along with leads to doing searches.

LINKS TO LAW SITES

FindLaw has been touted as being the best site to find other legal resources. Their Web page is available at:

http://www.findlaw.com/

Some of the links available on the FindLaw site include the following:

1. Consumer law
2. United States Supreme Court cases
3. State cases and laws

4. Law schools
5. Legal subject indexes
6. State law resources
7. Foreign and international resources
8. Law firms
9. Legal organizations
10. Government directories
11. Legal practice materials

If you are looking for a site on a law-related subject and do not know the Web site address, it is often easier to find the site on FindLaw than to do a search on your own. It is especially valuable if you are not sure exactly under which topic to conduct your key word search. The FindLaw Web site home page is shown in Figure 5-1.

FIGURE 5-1 Findlaw Web Site. Reprinted with permission from **Findlaw.com** © 1994–2002 FindLaw.

Lawyer Marketing
Advertising, Consultants, Strategies ...

Law Office & Practice
MY FindLaw, Free E-mail, Firm Web Sites ...

Students
Channel Home Page

Law Schools
Law Schools A-Z, Paralegals, Rankings ...

Law Reviews
General, International, Technology ...

Law Student Resources
Study Skills, Publications, Discussion Group ...

Pre-Law Resources
Financing, Preparation, Forums ...

Business
Channel Home Page

Business Formation
Business Plans, Legal Structure ...

Legal
Lawsuits, Contracts, Environmental ...

Finance
Bankruptcy, Funding, Taxes ...

Intellectual Property
Copyright, Patent, Trademark ...

Public
Channel Home Page

Housing
Landlord-Tenant, Buying, Selling ...

Auto
Accidents, Buying, Repairs ...

Personal Injury
Med Malpractice, Negligence, Products ...

Crime
Drunk Driving, Identity Theft ...

Government and Politics
Issues and Legislation, Write to Congress ...

Reference Resources
Library, Dictionary, Directories ...

Legal Organizations
Nat'l Bars, State Bars, Local Bars ...

Outlines & Exams
Const. Law, Civil Procedure, Property ...

Course Pages
Constitutional Law, Ethics, Evidence ...

Employment
Firm Salaries, Alt. Careers, Insider's Guide ...

The Bar
Prep-Courses, Bar Results, Bar Exams ...

Human Resources
Compensation, Hiring, Firing ...

Tech Deals & Contracts
Exec. Compensation, IP Licenses,
Acquisitions ...

Silicon Valley Center
Finance, Human Resources, Management ...

Lawyers
Lawyer Directory...

Family
Adoption, Divorce, Marriage ...

Money
Credit, Bankruptcy, Taxes, Wills ...

Work
Pensions, Termination ...

Immigration
Green Card, H1B, Student, Travel ...

Lawyers
Lawyer Directory...

TODAY IN WRIT
Natl. Railroad Passenger Corp. V. Morgan

The Supreme Court Considers The Continuing Violations Doctrine

by JOANNA GROSSMAN

MY Find Law

Email:

Password:

☐ Keep me logged in until I sign out.

Sign In

Forgot Your Password ? click here!

New User? Click Here!

FindLaw Newsletters
☑ **Legal Grounds**
Daily legal news.
☑ **US Supreme Court**
Case summaries.

Enter Email　　sign-up

more newsletters...

Community Boards
- Greedy Associates
- Divorce
- Employment Law
- Immigration Law
- Copyright Law
- Cyberspace Law
- Personal Injury

more boards...

Jobs @ FindLaw

Advertising Info - Awards - Disclaimer - Privacy - Company
Help & Information - Link to FindLaw - Comments - Add URL
Copyright © 1994-2002 FindLaw

FIGURE 5-1 *(continued)*

Some of the other sites that provide links to legal information may be found at:

http://www.ccglaw.com/links.htm

and

http://www.law.indiana.edu/law/v-lib/lawindex.html

The latter is called the World Wide Web Virtual Law Library and is arranged by subject. It includes links to sites of specialty areas of law, law firms, government resources, law journals, and search engines.

One site that provides three categories of information is located at:

http://law.net/roundnet.html

Links are available to legal resources, legal services, and attorneys by practice areas.

The University of Texas provides a legal resource guide on many different legal topics. This site may be found at:

http://uts.cc.utexas.edu/~juris

A comparable guide may be found at Cornell's Legal Information Institute at:

http://www.law.cornell.edu/lii.table.html

Infoseek's site provides links to many specialty practice areas, as well as links to international, federal, and state law. This site provides a searchable database and is located at:

http://www.guide-p.infoseek.com/Politics/Law

In addition to providing a large collection of links to law-related sites, the site provided by Legal Pad also provides legal clip art:

http://www.legal-pad.com/

The American Bar Association maintains a Legal Research Law Link that has links to all branches of government as well as the courts, Judicial Council, court home pages, law school libraries, and a number of other legal reference resources. It is located at:

http://www.abanet.org/lawlink/home.html

A large online catalog containing records for over 10 million holdings in libraries throughout the University of California system is the University of California's MELVYL home page, located at:

http://www.melvyl.ucop.edu/

LEGAL DOCUMENTS

Customized legal documents are provided at:

http://www.legaldocs.com/

This Web page enables the user to prepare customized documents on-line from templates. Some of these documents are free, and others have a small charge. Documents are available in the areas of wills, trusts, sales, leases, partnerships, employment, business, and real estate. Simple wills are available free of charge and may be prepared by completing a question-naire that is provided on the Web page. Remember that these documents are generic in nature; therefore, the state laws should always be reviewed for the state in which the document is being prepared to ascertain whether that document is valid in that particular state.

Court forms and pleadings from most states are available for downloading at the West Legal Studies Web site at:

http://www.westlegalstudies.com

LAW OFFICE TECHNOLOGY

A site that includes articles on technology and the legal effect thereof is located at:

http://tsw.ingress.com/tsw/ds/ds.html

KEY WORD SEARCHES

Searching by key word for legal resources is similar to general searches. Those who have used Westlaw or LEXIS are already familiar with key word searches.

Try to think of all the words that describe the material for which you are searching. Using a general term when you are looking for specific infor-mation yields too large a result. For instance, suppose you have a case on negligence and want to find information about the subject matter. Imagine the thousands of documents and cases that are available on the Internet containing the word "negligence." Narrow your search to a more definitive term, adding the state in which the case occurred, as well as any other spe-cific information required. As in computerized legal research systems, it is necessary to experiment with key words so that the result is neither too broad nor too narrow.

If you want the exact wording to be included at the site, then type the material in quotation marks. For instance, if you were looking for the case of *Roe v. Wade*, you would put "Roe v. Wade" in the search so that only that exact case will be found.

SUMMARY

This chapter encompasses the various legal sources for research on the Internet. Various search engines are available for finding legal information. Many legal resource guides are provided, along with lists of the subjects included. A site for customized legal documents is given. Court forms and pleadings are available for most states. Key word searches are described.

REVIEW QUESTIONS

1. Find this textbook on the Library of Congress Web page. How many books are listed by this author? Make a copy of the page giving that information.
2. List two Web sites that provide information about different areas of law.
3. What Web sites provide information on family law?
4. What site is useful if you are looking for a specific site on a subject in the legal area and do not know the Web site address?
5. What is MELVYL?

PRACTICAL PROBLEMS

1. Your attorney has asked you to find information about the Lemon Law in your state. Prepare a memorandum to the attorney with a definition of the law, how it is used, and the Web site on which the information was found.
2. List the key words you would use to find the following information in a key word search: Are individuals who wish to solicit money for

religious purposes protected under the United States Constitution if they wish to solicit at a shopping mall?

3. Your firm's client wishes to declare a homestead on his home, which he has transferred to his mother's name. He does, however, live in the house. May he legally declare this homestead? Where did you find the information?

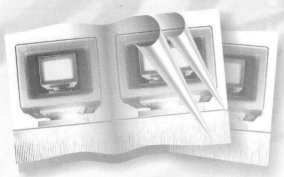

Federal Sources on the Internet

INTRODUCTION

Contacting federal agencies by telephone or regular mail may be difficult and time consuming. Spending the necessary time to reach the correct department or person is an arduous task. Most government agencies and departments are now available on the Web, and most give accurate and timely information on their sites. The federal courts, codes, and many cases are also available online. In this chapter, we will discuss the federal agencies available online along with their functions. The organization of the federal courts will be explained and their sites given. You will learn how to find federal cases and statutes.

FEDERAL GOVERNMENT

Government Agencies

Government Sources One of the most comprehensive listings of government sources on the Internet may be found at the Government Sources of Business and Economic Information at:

http://www.lib.umich.edu/00/inetdirrstacks/govdocs:tsangaustin

In addition to listing all government sources with Web pages, it provides an evaluation of each. Bear in mind, however, that the evaluations are subjective, and you may not agree with all assessments. With the number of government agencies establishing Web pages, it is often useful to be able to read an evaluation prior to doing your own search.

Aviation   Two government agencies are primarily responsible for information regarding airline accidents and incident reports. The National Transportation Safety Board (NTSB), located at:

http://www.ntsb.gov/aviation/aviation.htm

gives information helpful in aviation litigation, specifically information about airline crashes and incidents related to certain aircraft. Much of the information found on this page is available because of the Freedom of Information Act (FOIA). However, if requesting information via an FOIA form using regular mail, several weeks may pass before the information arrives. Much of the same information is available on the Web site.

The Federal Aviation Administration, whose Web page is located at:

http://www.faa.gov/

is responsible for the safety of civil aviation. As a component of the Department of Transportation, its functions include:

1. Regulating civil aviation to promote safety
2. Encourage development of air commerce and civil aeronautics
3. Develop and operate air traffic control and navigation systems for both civil and military aircraft
4. Develop and execute programs to control aircraft noise and other environmental effects of civil aviation
5. Regulate commercial space transportation[1]

Its activities include safety regulation of aircraft and airports, safe use of navigable airspace, construction or installation of visual and electronic aids to air navigation and their maintenance and operation, promotion of aviation safety abroad, regulation of commercial space transportation, and research and development of systems for a safe method of air navigation

---

[1] Federal Aviation Administration Web page, **http://www.faa.gov/**.

and air traffic control. The following additional information is available on the FAA Web site:

1. Agency policies
2. Regulations
3. Air traffic and safety
4. Regional offices and site maps
5. Commercial space transportation regulations
6. Civil aviation security

Both the NTSB and FAA sites are particularly helpful for those offices engaged in aviation litigation, particularly accident/incident reports and incidents involving certain types of aircraft and/or certain airlines.

Department of Transportation This federal department governs all transportation agencies of the government, including the FAA. Its Web site is located at:

http://www.dot.gov/

Links are available to the other divisions within the department, including the following:

1. FAA
2. Federal Highway Administration
3. Federal Railroad Administration
4. Federal Transit Administration
5. Maritime Administration
6. National Highway Traffic Safety Administration
7. United States Coast Guard

If the law office has a case that involves safety considerations on a federal highway or waterway, this site should be used.

State Department The secretary of state is appointed by the president, is the chief foreign affairs adviser, and oversees the State Department, which is the senior executive department of the United States government. Some of the activities of the department include:

1. Advice on foreign policy
2. Negotiations in foreign affairs
3. Grants and issues passports
4. Negotiation, interpretation, and termination of treaties
5. Assuring protection of United States citizens, property, and interests in foreign countries
6. Supervising immigration laws abroad
7. Providing information about travel conditions in foreign countries[2]

The State Department home page may be found at:

http://www.state.gov/index.html

This department also maintains a special page of travel advisories for individuals traveling to foreign countries, including those areas of political unrest or recent uprisings. The page was previously discussed in Chapter 4 and is available at:

http://travel.state.gov/travel_warnings.html

Consulting this page is particularly useful if an individual will be traveling to a foreign country. It should always be checked before making travel reservations abroad.

United States Census Bureau   Statistical information gathered from the census is available on this site:

http://www.census.gov/

It includes census data, financial data for government, economic, and population studies, and links to other sites.

Government Printing Office   Documents available from this office may be obtained from its Web site at:

http://www.access.gpo.gov/

Information is available about the intelligence community, Congress, Office of Special Counsel, General Accounting Office, Department of the

---

[2] United States State Department Web page, **http://www.state.gov/index.html**.

Interior, Executive Office of the President, and various other departments. Information from this site is particularly useful to a government law office or one that does business with the government.

The White House   In order to find this site on the Web, use the following address:

http://www2.whitehouse.gov/WH/Welcome.html

However, on many of the commercial services you may reach this site by merely keying:

white house

Information available at this site includes data on the president and vice president, the history of the White House and tour information, a library of press releases, radio addresses, and other related Web pages, summaries of today's press releases, the Constitution, and a considerable amount of material on current events. Cabinet offices and Executive Branch agencies are listed with addresses and telephone numbers at:

**http://www.whitehouse.gov/WH/Cabinet/html/
cabinet_links.html**

Central Intelligence Agency   The Director of the CIA heads the agencies that comprise the intelligence community of the United States. The CIA conducts investigations, surveillance, research, and other activities. The Web site is available at:

http://www.odci.gov/cia/

Their Web site describes the functions of the agency as well as providing links to readings about the intelligence community.

Federal Bureau of Investigation   The site for the FBI may be useful for those individuals who work in law offices that specialize in criminal law. The Web site is located at:

http://www.fbi.gov/

It includes information about the history of the FBI, programs available, speeches, press releases, chief investigations, the Most Wanted list, and other information.

Library of the House of Representatives An extensive law library, particularly valuable for federal sources, is available at the House of Representatives site at:

http://www.house.gov

The site also contains text of pending legislation as well as congressional testimony.

Immigration and Naturalization Service (INS) This organization is an agency of the Department of Justice and is responsible for the admission, naturalization, stopping of illegal entry, and deportation of foreigners. Their appeals board hears appeals to deportation orders.

Immigration laws change rapidly. Anyone employed in the area of immigration law should consult the INS Web site to obtain the latest rules and regulations. The Web site also contains forms that are in this specialty practice. It can be found at:

http://www.ins.usdoj.gov

Department of Justice This department manages the legal business of the United States. All federal law enforcement agencies are within the Department of Justice. It represents the United States in civil and criminal cases, runs the federal prison system, and has departments that are responsible for immigration (see INS), antitrust, civil rights, the Federal Bureau of Investigation (see FBI), the Drug Enforcement Administration (DEA), and a number of other agencies. It is headed by the attorney general of the United States. The Web site is located at:

http://www.usdoj.gov

and includes information on the various agencies in the department, recent case decisions involving the justice department, and other information related to the United States legal community. This site is particularly useful for criminal law practices, particularly in the areas of drug-related offenses, federal crimes, and racketeering.

Department of Commerce/Patent and Trademark Office Patent attorneys and paralegals will find this site particularly valuable for obtaining information about trademarks and patents. Forms are provided to register and maintain trademarks and patents. There are links to related sites. The site may be found at:

http://www.uspto.gov

Internal Revenue Service A considerable amount of tax information is provided at the IRS site at:

http://www.irs.ustreas.gov

Tax forms may be downloaded from the site. Publications on IRS regulations are also available for downloading.

Department of Labor The Department of Labor regulates working conditions, manpower development, and labor-management relations. Its Web site contains information on wages, hours of employment, workplace issues, and running small businesses. It includes federal labor regulations and is located at:

http://www.dol.gov

Securities and Exchange Commission (SEC) The SEC is responsible for administering the federal and state laws that regulate the sale of securities. Included on the site are the Securities Act of 1933, which requires the registration of securities to be sold to the public and the disclosure of complete information to possible buyers; the Securities and Exchange Act of 1934, which regulates both stock exchanges and sales of stock over the counter; and other information related to the purchase and sale of securities. Its Web site is particularly useful for those law offices specializing in corporate law and is located at:

http://www.sec.gov/

The Web site provides a method for filing online, information on other corporate filings, a database to search for information on filings, information for small businesses, and current rules and regulations.

Social Security Administration This Web site provides access to your personal earnings as well as future benefits estimates. Information is provided about Social Security benefits and Medicare. Explanations are given for the system's regulations. The site is available at:

http://www.ssa.gov/SSA_Home.html

Those law firms that deal in elder law or Social Security law will find this site particularly useful.

Library of Congress Many additional departments and agencies exist in the federal government that are not listed here. For those departments not listed, the best place to find listings of federal, state, and local governments and agencies is on the Library of Congress page, which provides links to other government departments. The page may be found at:

http://www.lcweb.loc.gov/

FEDERAL COURTS

The Federal courts are divided into the following general areas:

1. United States Supreme Court
2. Circuit Courts of Appeal
3. Federal District Courts

United States Supreme Court

The Supreme Court of the United States is the highest court in the land. It is located in Washington, D.C. and sits from the first Monday in October until the end of May. Nine justices sit on the court, one of whom is the Chief Justice, who presides over the Court. All decisions of the Federal Circuit Courts of Appeal may be appealed to the Supreme Court. It may also hear cases where the highest state court has issued a decision that challenges the validity of a federal law. Generally, the Court only hears cases that raise significant issues and declines to hear the majority of cases referred to it. Various Web sites exist for different areas of the Supreme Court as indicated:

1. Current Court Calendar
   http://supct.law.cornell.edu/supct/calendar.html

2. Oral Arguments
   http://supct.law.cornell.edu/supct/argcal97.html

3. Case Name Search
   http://www.fedworld.gov/supcourt/csearch.htm

   This site is useful if you know the names of the parties to the action but do not have the complete citation.

4. FindLaw Web Page for Supreme Court Cases and the United States Code
   http://www.findlaw.com/casecode/supreme.html

5. Cases from 1967–Present
   http://www.ljextra.com/cgi-bin/ussc

6. Supreme Court Cases
   http://www.usscplus.com/research.shtml

   This site also includes oral arguments in Real Audio and the federal judiciary home page.

7. Supreme Court Rules
   http://www.law.cornell.edu/rules/supct/overview.html

The Federal Legal Information Through Electronics (FLITE) database includes over 7,000 Supreme Court cases from 1937 through 1975. Volumes 300 through 422 of the United States Reports are included in this database. If the case in which you are interested was decided during that time period and you know the name and citation number, you may access the following Web site to find the case:

http://www.fedworld.gov/supcourt/index.htm

If you would like to do a key word search and do not know the name or citation number of the case, use this Web site:

http://www.fedworld.gov/supcourt/fsearch.htm

Circuit Courts of Appeal

The intermediary federal court for appeals are the Circuit Courts of Appeal, which hear cases appealed from the United States District Courts. The thirteen circuits each represent several states and the federal system.

Twelve regional circuits represent intermediate courts of appeal. They hear appeals from the United States District Courts in each state, bankruptcy courts, the Tax Court, and the Administrative Agency Tribunal.

The United States Court of Appeals for the Federal Circuit represents federal appeals from the Court of Claims, Court of International Trade, Court of Veterans Appeals, Patents and Trademarks, and other courts with special jurisdiction. The number of justices in each circuit varies by the size of the court and the number of cases being heard.

Several sources exist for finding cases from the circuit courts. General sources for all circuits may be found at:

http://www.law.vill.edu/Fed-Ct/fedcourt.html

This Web page includes federal court opinions, Supreme Court rules, Appeals Court rules, and rules from some states and federal agencies.

FEDERAL COURT OPINIONS

Federal Circuit Courts of Appeal

A number of sources for finding opinions of the circuit courts are listed below:

http://search.ljx.com
http://www.ljextra.com/cgi-bin/cir
http://www.ll.georgetown.edu/Fed-Ct/Circuit/fed/search.html
http://www.law.emory.edu/fedcircuit/fedcasearch.html
http://www.law.vill.edu/Fed-Ct/fedcourt.html

Some law schools also have online libraries of appellate court opinions within individual districts. The list of Web sites is as follows:

1. First Circuit
   http://www.law.emory.edu/1circuit/
   http://www.law.emory.edu/1circuit/1casearch.html
2. Second Circuit
   http://www.tourolaw.edu/2ndcircuit/
   http://www.law.pace.edu/legal/us-legal/judiciary/
      second-circuit.html
3. Third Circuit
   http://www.law.vill.edu/Fed-Ct/ca03.html

   4. Fourth Circuit
      http://www.law.emory.edu/4circuit/

   5. Fifth Circuit
      **http://www.ca5.uscourts.gov/www.law.utexas.edu/us5th/
      us5th.html**

   6. Sixth Circuit
      http://www.law.emory.edu/6circuit/

   7. Seventh Circuit
      http://www.law.emory.edu/7circuit/7casearch.html

   8. Eighth Circuit
      http://www.wulaw.wustl.edu/8th.cir/opinions.html

   9. Ninth Circuit
      http://www.ce9.uscourts.gov

  10. Tenth Circuit
      http://www.emory.edu/10circuit

  11. Eleventh Circuit
      http://www.emory.edu/11circuit

  12. Federal Circuit
      http://www.fedcir.gov/
      http://www.ll.georgetown.edu/Fed-Ct/Circuit/fed/

Some of these Web sites also include district court and bankruptcy court decisions for the specific circuit. Gateway sites, such as FindLaw, also provide links to these courts.

Federal District Courts

The United States District Courts are the trial courts on the federal level. There are 94 federal judicial districts, with at least one in each state. Larger and heavily populated states have several districts. Most cases heard in these courts involve questions of federal law, such as statutes, treaties, or the Constitution. Cases against the United States government, cases involving diversity of citizenship (where the plaintiff and defendant reside in different states and the amount in controversy is over the current minimum), and cases in specialized areas such as customs and admiralty also come under the original jurisdiction of the district courts. Federal crimes, such as racketeering, security fraud, bank robbery, mail fraud, certain drug-related crimes, and kidnapping, are also prosecuted in these courts.

The various states generally list the court opinions and rules on the state court Web pages. Therefore, the Web pages will be listed under each state's pages. A general Web page for the federal courts is available at:

http://www.uscourts.gov/

This page is the home page of the federal judiciary and includes information about the courts, opinions, and court news.

FEDERAL STATUTES AND COURT RULES————

Federal Court Rules

The rules for the federal courts are available in the United States Codes, *supra*. The appendix to Title 28 of the United States Code contains the Federal Rules of Evidence, Appellate, and Civil Procedure. The appendix to Title 18 of the U.S. Code contains the Federal Rules of Criminal Procedure. The Federal Rules of Evidence are also found at:

http://www.law.cornell.edu/rules/fre/overview.html

Federal Rules of Civil Procedure

The Rules of Civil Procedure set out the procedural rules that must be followed in the federal courts. In this Web page:

http://www.law.cornell.edu/rules/frcp/overview.htm

all of the rules and articles may be found by key word search. For example, if you are interested in specific filing requirements, use the key words "filing requirements Texas" and you should be able to reach the appropriate material. This Web page also provides links to proposed changes in these rules as well as other documents that have been written about the specific rules.

Web pages for specific federal rules are:

1. Federal Rules of Civil Procedure
    http://www.law.cornell.edu/rules/frcp/overview.html

   2. Federal Rules of Evidence
      http://www.law.cornell.edu/rules/fre/overview.html

If the federal rule is confusing or obscure, use one of the treatises available:

   1. *Moore's Federal Practice*—Federal courts
   2. *Federal Practice and Procedure*—Federal courts practice
   3. *McCormick on Evidence* or *Weinstein's Evidence*—Federal Rules of Evidence

Local federal court rules may be available at the Federal District Court Web page for your state.

United States Code

The United States Code is arranged in Titles, beginning with the General Provisions (Title 1) and continuing alphabetically to the last title, which is War and National Defense (Title 50). The Web page to access all 50 titles may be found at:

http://www.law.cornell.edu/uscode/

Each code is further divided into various sections and chapters. This page enables one to search by several different methods, including the following:

   1. Title and chapter
   2. Title alone
   3. By popular name of the law
   4. By sections of the individual title
   5. By table of contents to the Code

It should be noted that several different federal sources are available at the following general site:

http://www.law.cornell.edu/

The Federal Rules of Civil Procedure are available on that site at:

http://www.law.cornell.edu/rules/frcp/overview.html

and the Federal Rules of Evidence may be accessed at:

http://www.law.cornell.edu/rules/fre/overview.html

Updating of the codes and rules is not generally reliable. If the latest section is required, be sure to check the date and the advance sheets as well.

Federal Justices

Information about the justices of the federal courts, as well as several other examples of information about the federal system, may be found at:

http://www.legal.gas.gov/

This is a general federal site that also provides information about statutes, regulations, state laws, professional associations, arbitration, mediation, and links to other legal sites.

SUMMARY

This chapter furnishes a synopsis of the federal government sites available. Descriptions of each are provided. Federal courts, codes, and agencies are discussed.

REVIEW QUESTIONS

Match the government agency with its function.

1. National Transportation Safety Board
2. Department of State
3. Department of Transportation
4. Immigration and Naturalization Service
5. Department of Justice

a. Responsible for deportation of foreigners
b. Manages legal business of the United States
c. Investigates airline accidents
d. Negotiates treaties
e. Governs transportation agencies

PRACTICAL PROBLEMS

1. Find the federal statute with the definition of "racketeering." Indicate the Web page of the definition as well as the definition itself.

2. Find the Web page for the State Department. List the duties and responsibilities of the secretary of state.

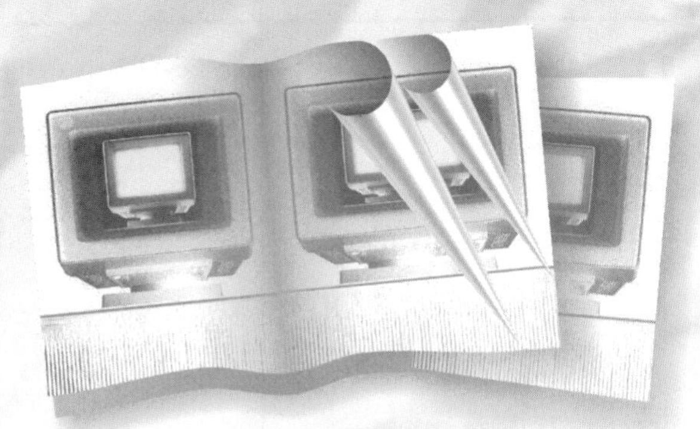

CHAPTER 7

State Sources on the Internet

INTRODUCTION

State agencies and state government offices are often difficult to reach by telephone. Spending the necessary time to finally reach the correct department or person is often frustrating. However, many state agencies and departments are now available on the Internet, and most give accurate and timely information on their sites. In this chapter, we will address the various Web sites available for state offices and state legal sources.

STATE GOVERNMENT OFFICES

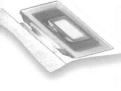

The number of Web sites available that provide information on state government offices is very large. Instead of providing Web page addresses for all fifty states, the Web pages that provide links to the different states are listed below. These particular links supply information about not only state government offices, but also about statutes, law reviews, publishers, and other law-related material.

One of the most comprehensive sites for this purpose is:

http://www.findlaw.com/

FindLaw provides a great number of sources for legal research, including the following:

1. Federal government sources
2. Legal news

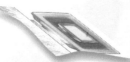

3. Law reviews

4. Statutes

5. Law schools

6. Cases

7. Professional legal organizations

8. Experts in various specialty fields

9. International legal sources

One source that provides a relatively fast method of linking to state and federal law sources, including state codes, is:

http://www.lawsonline.com/

STATE COURTS AND CASES

Many different state courts have their own Web pages. A site where links to those state courts, as well as the court opinions, may be found is:

http://www.law.vill.edu/State-Ct/index.html

Another excellent link to material on the Web is the World Wide Web Virtual Law Library, which can be found at:

http://www.law.indiana.edu/law/v-lib/lawindex.html

Not only does this library provide information on state sources, but it also provides links to many different specialty areas of the law, including business law, family law, labor law, torts, taxation, criminal law, and many others. It links to other sites listing additional legal resources available on the Web. In some cases, this library is an excellent starting point for legal research on the Web.

Some additional sites that provide links and indexes to state law on the Internet follow:

http://law.house.gov/17.htm
http://www.prairienet.org/~scruffy/f.htm
http://www.law.indiana.edu/law/v-lib/states.html

State of California

California provides an extensive number of Internet sites for state government, codes, and cases. Following are some of the more noteworthy of these sites:

Computer Aided Le...

The proper methods of citing cases may be found i...
located at:

www.law.cornell.edu/citation/cit...

SHEPARDIZING

Shepard's lists relevant cases a...
cision is handed down from...
particular statute or case...
case. It tells whether...
most critical nota...
and are citing...
the cases ci...
In *Sh...
ate v...
pa...

...information.

State government and state court sites are also accessible via a link at:

www.westlegalstudies.com

CITATIONS

All cases have their own "address," known as a citation. The citation gives the volume number, series, and page number on which the case is located. For example, 45 U.S. 222 may be found in volume 45 of United States Reports on page 222.

an online textbook

tion.table.html

nd other material that occur after a case de-
the courts and that has a direct bearing on that
. It lists all subsequent cases that cite the subject
a case has been followed or overruled, which is the
on. If you are preparing a legal document for the courts
elevant cases to support your point of view, it is critical that
ed have not been overruled.
pard's the subject case may be found by looking in the appropri-
lumes for that particular series, then numerically by volume, then by
ge number. *Shepard's* lists almost every case and statute in the United
States. "Shepardizing" refers to determining whether the subject case has
been overruled by a later case by looking it up in *Shepard's Citations.*
Shepard's is also useful for tracing the history of a case. More information
on *Shepard's* is available online at:

http://shepards.com/ccentral/tutorial/content1.htm

WESTLAW AND LEXIS

The all-encompassing computerized legal research systems are also available online for a fee. They may be accessed on the Internet via their re-
spective Web pages. A password must be entered to gain access to the
database; time using the database is computed automatically. These sites
are located at:

http://www.westlaw.com

http://www.lexis.com

Additional sources are also available on the Web pages. For instance,
West's Legal Directory of Attorneys may be accessed through the address
above.

A detailed description for using the Westlaw and LEXIS systems will be provided in Chapter 10.

PLEADINGS AND FORMS

A number of different sites make forms and documents available on the Web. In addition, many attorneys who have their own Web pages provide documents and forms, some free and some for a fee. Some forms may be obtained from the West Legal Studies Web page at:

http://www.westlegalstudies.com

California uses many judicial council forms that are available on the state Web page and from the following site as well:

http://www.LawCA.com/JC.htm

Some of these forms and documents are free; others are provided for a fee. The latter Web site provides the ability to download forms from the site itself. Some legal areas whose associated forms are available at this site include:

1. Name change
2. Eviction
3. Orders
4. Dissolution
5. Bankruptcy

Some of the federal sites described in this chapter have links to sites that provide forms and documents.

A general site for legal forms may be accessed at:

http://lawlib.wuacc.edu/washlaw/legalforms/legalforms.html

SUMMARY

In this chapter, the state agencies and government offices are discussed. The Web sites for other legal sources on the state level are also provided. Methods of searching for state court cases and documents are discussed and various Web addresses listed.

REVIEW QUESTIONS

1. Find the codes for your state. Indicate the Web address.
2. What Web site would you use to find the appellate and supreme court decisions from your state? Are they available on the Internet?
3. Which site would you use for a link to your state's government offices?
4. What is provided at the Web site for the World Wide Web Virtual Law Library?
5. What is a citation? Give an example of a citation from your state's appellate court.

PRACTICAL PROBLEMS

1. Your firm is working on a case involving murder with special circumstances. Does your state recognize capital punishment? If so, under what circumstances? Prepare a memorandum to the attorney describing this information.
2. Find five government agencies in your state that have Web pages. Indicate the name of the agency, the Web page address, and the agency's functions.

CHAPTER 8

Secondary Sources and Finding Tools on the Internet

INTRODUCTION

In the previous chapters we learned about the primary sources (primary authority) used in the federal and state areas of information. By definition, primary sources represent the "law" in your particular jurisdiction. They present authority that is binding on the courts and include laws (codes and statutes), court decisions, administrative regulations, constitutions, and other sources of law as opposed to interpretive or indirect information from legal encyclopedias, treatises, textbooks, or other secondary sources.

Secondary sources are useful for learning about the law and for finding other material as well as locating primary sources. They represent persuasive authority that a judge or justice might use, but is not required to use. Such sources include legal encyclopedias and cases or statutes from other jurisdictions. For example, in deciding a case in California, a judge may look at persuasive authority on the laws of other states; however, he must use cases in his jurisdiction in California in reaching a decision.

Secondary sources may be found online in law library and college library catalogs. In some cases, legal encyclopedias are available online. Law review articles often provide useful information and citations to cases in your own jurisdiction.

LAW SCHOOLS AND THEIR LIBRARIES

The complete list of law schools and their libraries available online is too large to put into a book format. It is advisable to do your own search for law schools and their libraries if the particular school is not listed here. In most cases, the site address for the law school and its library are listed as separate sites. Each law school site provides particular information about the individual law school, such as academic services, faculty, placement activities, courses offered, and admissions requirements. Individual law school sites provide links to their own libraries.

Case Western Reserve University—Ohio

Both the law school and its library are available online. To go directly to the law school, find:

http://lawwww.cwru.edu/

To go directly to the library, find:

http://lawwww.cwru.edu/cwrulaw/library/libinfo.html

In addition to general information about the law school itself, this site provides links to other legal reference materials, as well as publications and research by the law school students and professors.

The library page provides a guide to Case Western's law library as well as online catalogs of library materials, links to other law school libraries, and the location of their basic legal research information.

Chicago-Kent College of Law/Library

This law school and library offers one of the best sites for finding links and information about any of the law libraries available online. In addition to providing information about its own law school, links to various county departments are included. Their law review is available online. Decisions of the Illinois Human Rights Commission are provided.

The law school is available at:

http://www.kentlaw.edu/

The law library is available at:

http://www.infoctr.edu/lawlib/

Cornell University—Law School/Library

Perhaps the largest provider of links to applicable legal research sites, Cornell provides their law school Web page as well as sites for the law library and the Legal Information Institute. Their addresses are:

Law school:
http://www.law.cornell.edu/admit/admit.htm

Law library:
http://www.law.cornell.edu/library/default.html

Legal Information Institute:
http://www.law.cornell.edu:80/lii.table.html

The law school provides extensive information about the school as well as law reviews and studies undertaken at the law school. The law library's page provides an extensive legal research encyclopedia, a Global Legal Information Network dealing with international law sources, research guides, and law journals.

The Legal Information Institute has links to various government agency Web pages. Since the Institute provides one of the largest number of legal research links available, this is an excellent place to begin your legal research. Access to the Supreme Court's most recent decisions are also available at this site. The decisions may be accessed by using one of five search methods:

1. The full citation
2. A topical index
3. A key word search
4. Indices of the names of parties by the year of the decision
5. By date of decision (for the most recent term only)

A gallery is provided of the Supreme Court Justices with biographical information and pictures of all of the justices, along with links to the opinions written by each justice, including concurring and dissenting opinions.

Emory University—Law School/Library

This site provides access to links to many federal circuit court decisions and other documents available on the Web. It also has access to information on legal materials in Georgia and provides a research aid as well.

The law school can be found at:

http://www.olaw.emory.edu/

The library can be found at:

http://www.law.emory.edu/LAW/law.html

Harvard Law School/Library

Most of the information on this site relates to the law school itself. Very few links are provided for other research capabilities. The law school site gives extensive information about classes, professors, admissions, alumni, students, and special events. The library site primarily gives information about sources available at Harvard itself. These sites may be found at:

Law school:
http://www.law.harvard.edu/

Law library:
http://www.law.harvard.edu/library/

Indiana University Law School/Library

An excellent source for a tremendous amount of legal research materials and links is available at:

http://www.law.indiana.edu

This site is updated frequently and can be depended on to have up-to-date information and the most current links available.

University of Chicago Law School/D'Angelo Law Library

A considerable amount of information about both the law school and many law sites are available here. It is also home to the Center for the Study of Constitutionalism in Eastern Europe. It contains links to many federal sources, including cases, courts, and government agencies. The sites are found at:

School:
http://www-law.lib.uchicago.edu/

Library:
http://www-law.lib.uchicago.edu/lib/

Space does not allow the listing of every law library with a Web site. However, most major law schools in the United States provide Web sites for both their schools and libraries. If a law school is not listed here, then conduct a search of law schools to find the one for which you are looking. The FindLaw site also provides links to law schools.

LEGAL DICTIONARY

Legal dictionaries are easy to find online. A good site to look for words on a world-wide basis may be found at:

http://www.duhaime.org/diction.htm

LEGAL RESEARCH QUESTIONS

Encyclopedia Britannica

While this encyclopedia is not a legal encyclopedia per se, it does contain thousands of sources of interest. It identifies the best sites for hundreds of subject areas and is available by subscription at:

http://www.eb.com/

Westlaw

Users of the Westlaw service have their own listserv, available by subscription by an e-mail to:

listserv@lawlib.wuacc.edu
Subject: (any)
Message: **subscribe westlawuser-l Jlong** (or your screen name)

Westlaw users discuss pertinent issues and items related to the Westlaw database.

Prior discussions may be found at:
http://www.ftplaw.wuacc.edu/listproc/westlawuser-l/
Information about a subscription to Westlaw may be obtained at:
http://www.westlaw.com

which is the official site for Westlaw. You may also access Westlaw from this site if you have an existing account.

Virtual Legal Search Engine

In order to find a site that provides a number of different links to other legal information, go to the Virtual Legal Search Engine located at:

http://www.virtualfreesites.com/search.legal.html

This site provides a list of links to many legal sites, some of which have been discussed. If you are not certain which site to use for your search, this site may be a good place to start.

Law-Related Listservs

As discussed earlier, listservs represent a means for an individual to subscribe to a discussion group that sends e-mail to a number of people about different topics. Once you subscribe to the listserv, your e-mail address becomes part of their database. When someone sends an e-mail to the list, all members receive a copy. If you wish to respond to the e-mail, your reply is sent to the group. Often valuable information may be obtained about legal issues.

For instance, when the author was writing this textbook, she asked the members of the paralegal educators' listserv about legal links they may have used and found to be valuable in teaching legal research. Many of their suggestions are included herein.

One particularly valuable listserv actually contains lists of other listservs, journals, law firms on the net, and bulletin boards that might be of interest to the legal profession. You may join this listserv by sending an e-mail with the following information:

TO:	**listserv@justice.eliot.me.us**
FROM:	<your screen name>
SUBJECT:	legal list
BODY:	Subscribe LEGAL-LIST <your screen name>

Once you join any listserv, you will continue to receive all e-mail distributed thereon until you unsubscribe. After you join, an e-mail will be sent to you with information on how to post messages and how to unsubscribe. Be sure to keep this e-mail in your files in the event you decide at some future time that you are no longer interested in receiving e-mail from the list.

An excellent source for obtaining lists of all accessible legal listservs is available at:

http://www.wls.lib.ny.us/resources/legallistservs.html

This site provides information about over 400 legal lists that you may join as well as a number of different newsgroups on legal topics.

One particularly valuable list is aimed at the exchange of information about law-related Internet resources. Subscribing to this list will assure the receipt of every announcement of new or updated law-related resources. Discussions are also provided on the merits of various sites and questions are asked and answered about how to find a particular topic. If you do a considerable amount of legal research on the Internet and wish to keep abreast of all of the latest developments on new sites, it would be beneficial to join this list. The following e-mail will enter a subscription to this list:

TO: **listserv@listserv.law.cornell.edu**
FROM: <your screen name>
SUBJECT: list <or any other topic>
BODY: Subscribe LAWSRC-L <your screen name>

One relatively new list that is comprised primarily of attorneys who are new to using the Internet for legal research is called NET-LAWYERS. Individuals share their discovery of new sites and critique various sites. People ask and answer questions about where to find certain items. Although the site is largely made by and for attorneys, it is valuable for anyone who does legal research on the Internet. You may join by sending the following e-mail:

TO: **net-lawyers-request@webcom.com**
FROM: <your screen name>
BODY: Subscribe <your screen name>

LAW FIRMS AND ATTORNEYS

Many private attorneys and law firms have their own Web pages. The best way to find a specific law firm's Web page is to do a search using the name of the firm in quotation marks. For example, using one of the search engines described earlier, key the name of the law firm within quotation marks into the search box. If that firm has a Web page, its location should be displayed. If you are not certain of the firm's full name, then key in the name as you think it is without the quotation marks. If you know the name of the firm, you would key:

"Long Law Firm"

If you are not sure of the name of the firm, you would key:

Long Law Firm

West Legal Directory

The *West Legal Directory* represents biographical listings of over one million lawyers. Searches are possible by subject, practice area, notable characteristics or attributes of the attorney, and location. For example, you could actually search for "a French-speaking immigration attorney in Chicago." It is possible to search for the following subjects in the *West Legal Directory,* accessible at:

http://www.lawoffice.com/

1. Search by name
2. United States lawyers
3. International counsel
4. Corporate lawyers
5. Government lawyers
6. United States courts
7. Law students
8. Lawyer services guides
9. Areas of law
10. State law information
11. Overview of the United States courts
12. Law dictionary
13. Articles from different law firms
14. How to hire a lawyer

In addition, every day articles from law firms are featured by provided links. Figure 8-1 shows the home page of the *West Legal Directory.*

A locator service for attorneys can be found at:

http://www.attorneyfind.com/

This site enables you to search for law firms and lawyers in different states and in different specialty areas.

Most people who have worked in law offices are familiar with the *Martindale-Hubbell Legal Directory of Attorneys and Law Firms*. This same directory is now provided online at:

http://www.martindale.com

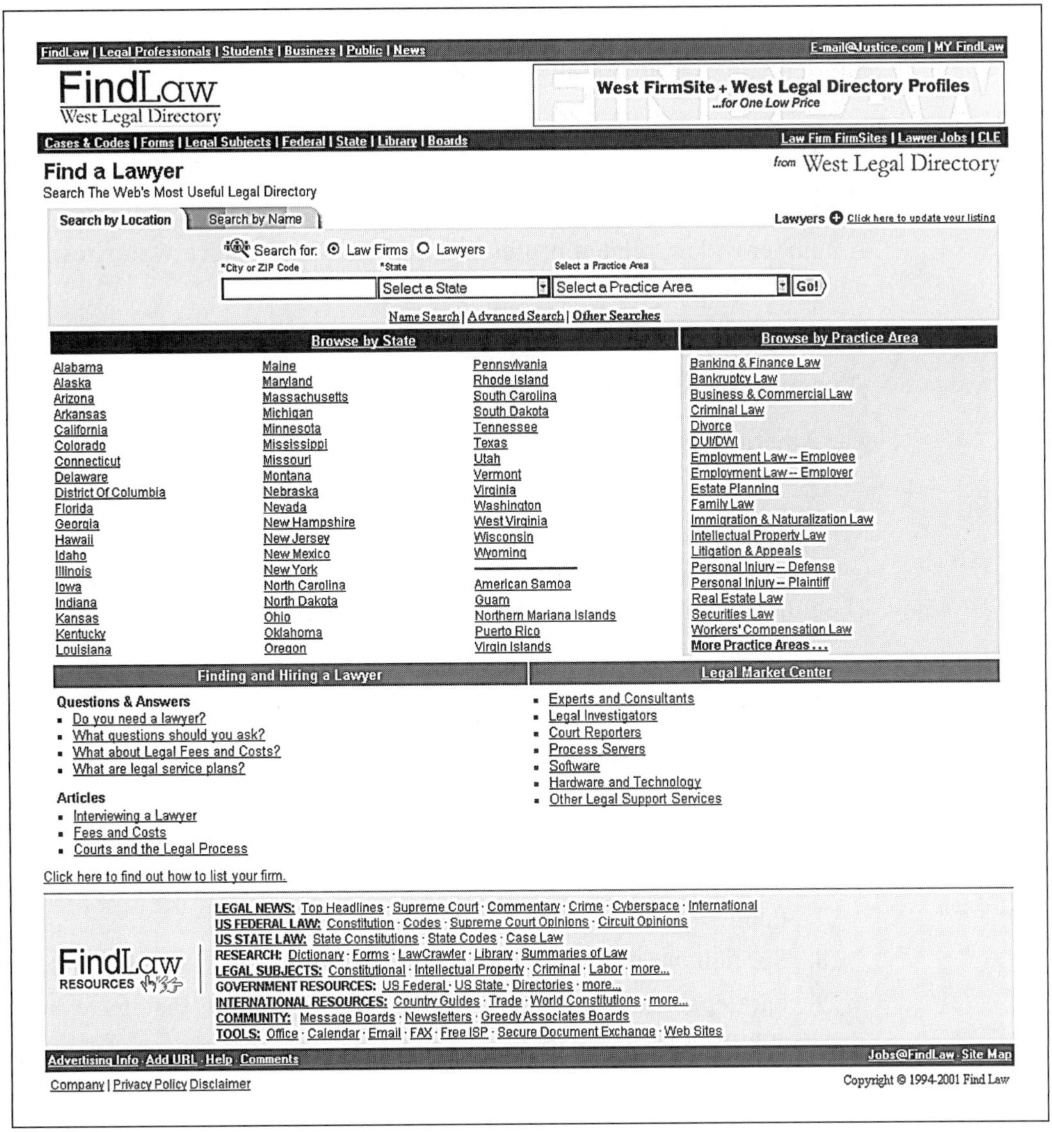

FIGURE 8-1 West Legal Directory Home Page. Reprinted with permission from *West Legal Directory* online © 2002 West Group.

This directory includes over 900,000 listings of law firms and attorneys in the United States and other parts of the world. Searches are possible by name, city, state, country, language, and province. It is also possible to search here for government attorneys and corporate law departments. Individual listings for attorneys include their name, address, telephone number, areas of practice, educational background, professional affiliations, and sometimes representative clients.

PROFESSIONAL ORGANIZATIONS

A number of law-related professional organizations have Web sites. The most frequently used are listed in this section.

American Bar Association

The American Bar Association (ABA) maintains its Web site at:

http://www.abanet.org/

In addition to providing information about the organization for its members, a considerable number of other items are also included on the site. The following is a representative list of information available:

1. Membership information
2. Publications of the ABA
3. Continuing Legal Education issues
4. The *ABA Journal*
5. Links to other law-related sites
6. Information about the legal community
7. Public information about the legal profession
8. Specialty sections and news about upcoming events
9. Paralegal information, including those schools that have been approved by the ABA

State Bar Organizations

Space does not permit the listing of all state bar organizations in the country. However, a search may be conducted to find your own state's bar organization by doing a key word search. When you establish the search engine, key into the space for key words:

"Indiana State Bar"   or   Indiana State Bar

or whatever state's bar organization is the object of your research.

Paralegal Organizations

A number of paralegal organizations exist both on the local and national level. Probably the largest local paralegal organization in the country is the Los Angeles Paralegal Association (LAPA), with 1,100 members in the greater Los Angeles metropolitan region. Its site can be found at:

http://www.lapa.org

The organization is dedicated to the development of the paralegal profession and provides opportunities for professional development and networking. The site maintains information about meetings and upcoming events. It also has links to monthly publication information, member benefits, specialty groups, and specialty services for members, including résumé bank for job searching, membership directory, annual employment and salary survey, paralegal schools list, and a job hunting handbook. Students may join LAPA for a reduced fee.

The National Association for Legal Assistants (NALA) is a leading national professional association for paralegals. Its site may be found at:

http://www.nala.org

This association provides continuing education and professional certification programs for paralegals. NALA was incorporated in 1975 and is one of the oldest paralegal organizations in the United States. The site contains information about its quarterly journal, *Facts and Findings*. It also provides an online campus offering classes and seminars. The Internet campus was developed by West Publishing Company and NALA for legal professionals. Classes are available for the Certified Legal Assistant examination, continuing legal education, and paralegal skills. Classes presently offered include Communications, Judgment and Legal Analysis, and Legal Research.

This site also provides links to vendors and other professional legal organizations, including:

1. American Law Institute—American Bar Association Committee
2. Association of Legal Administrators

3. American Association for Paralegal Education (paralegal educators)

4. Corporate Law Department

5. National Notary Association

6. Legal Assistants Division of the State Bar of Texas

A link is provided to the *American Standard Dictionary* and to Information America, which searches public records free or for a nominal fee.

Another national organization in the paralegal area is the National Federation of Paralegal Associations (NFPA) located at:

http://www.paralegals.org

This is their main Web page. It contains links to state and federal statutes as well as many other sites of interest to paralegals.

NFPA's main Web page provides links to press releases, surveys, news, legal research sources, products, services, a calendar, a career center for paralegals, articles on getting started in the paralegal profession, membership information, the *National Paralegal Reporter* publication, professional development, the paralegal advanced competency examination, networking (listservs and chat rooms), publications, international information, continuing legal education online, *pro bono* activities, and opportunities in the field.

Their legal research links include:

1. Federal agencies

2. Federal departments

3. Federal statutes and cases

4. State agencies and departments

5. State statutes and cases

6. State and federal courts

7. International law

8. Internet directories and search engines

9. Sites for specialty practice

10. Organization and association links

11. Listservs and law-related forums

12. Law schools and research centers

They maintain eighteen listservs, most of which are for members only, including:

1. Bankruptcy/collections
2. Corporate law
3. Corporate litigation department paralegals
4. Criminal law
5. Educators
6. Family law
7. Freelance paralegals
8. General discussion
9. Immigration
10. Labor law
11. Law office management
12. Litigation
13. Independent paralegals
14. Intellectual property
15. Probate, estates, and trusts
16. Real estate law
17. Students
18. Technology

The American Association for Paralegal Education (AAFPE) is a national organization serving paralegal education and institutions offering paralegal education programs. Its site, located at:

http://www.aafpe.org

includes information on paralegal programs throughout the country, as well as membership, educational resources, association links, and news for paralegal educators. It contains articles from the *Journal.* An Internet discussion list and a list of state bar associations and publishers are provided. The page contains an article on how to choose a paralegal program. A membership directory that can be searched is provided along with e-mail links to program directors at member colleges and universities.

The Association of Legal Administrators (ALA) provides its Web site at:

http://www.alanet.org/

This group's mission is to improve the quality of management in legal services organizations, promote and enhance the competence and professionalism of legal administrators and management, and represent professional legal management in the community.[1]

Some items on this site are available to members of the organization only. The following information is provided:

1. Links to annual education conference
2. Association news
3. Career information
4. Industry digests
5. Available documents
6. Online discussion group
7. Continuing professional education
8. Association and legal management industry news
9. Membership information

Many law office employees also become notary publics. The Web site for the National Notary Association is located at:

http://www.nationalnotary.org

The National Association of Legal Secretaries (NALS) has a national office and branches throughout the country. Their main site is located at:

http://www.nals.org/

Their Web page has links to other legal resources, membership information, legal news applicable to legal secretaries, a chat room, and a description of the advantages and benefits of their organization. Some state branches also have their own Web sites.

COLLEGES

Most colleges throughout the United States offer pre-law, paralegal, and legal secretarial programs. The list is so extensive that it would be

---

[1] Association of Legal Administrators' Web Page; home page; **http://www.alanet.org/**.

wise to do a search for a program in your own state. Information and recommendations about different programs may be obtained from your state bar association, the site for the American Association for Paralegal Education (discussed above), the National Association of Legal Assistants, and the National Association of Legal Secretaries. All of these Web sites have been previously discussed in this chapter.

Law schools were discussed in a previous chapter and their Web sites noted. Investigate the ABA site and your state bar association's site for information on choosing a law school. The ABA also has a section for legal assistants (paralegals) that approves paralegal programs throughout the country. Information about this procedure may be found on their site (**http://www.abanet.org/**), which also provides a list of those paralegal programs approved by the ABA.

Many local and statewide professional organizations exist in the legal area; they are too numerous to list here. However, you now have the tools to search the Internet to find the type of schools that are of interest to you.

SUMMARY

This chapter provides secondary sources that are useful for learning about the law and for finding other material. A number of law school library sites are given. Web site information is listed for professional organizations, including state bar associations and organizations for paralegals, paralegal education, legal secretaries, and legal administrators.

REVIEW QUESTIONS

1. Give three examples of secondary sources.
2. What is the Web site for the Legal Information Institute at Cornell University?
3. Where would you find information about admission to Harvard Law School?
4. List two online legal dictionaries.
5. How would you subscribe to the Westlaw listserv?

PRACTICAL PROBLEMS

1. Write a memorandum to the attorney about your state's interpretation of the property rights in military pensions. Your client is a retired admiral in the Navy and is divorcing his spouse of 25 years. He retired after 30 years of service last year. Will he have to share his pension with his ex-wife? If so, what percentage will he keep, and what percentage will she get? *Hint:* Look in recent law review articles for interpretation of this federal law.

2. Join a legal listserv and send a copy of the e-mail joining the listserv to your instructor.

3. Post a message on the listserv you joined in problem 2 and send a copy to your instructor.

CHAPTER 9

Specialized Areas of Law on the Internet

INTRODUCTION

This chapter will describe some of the more common areas of specialty for law offices and, in each section, list and describe the sites related to those particular topics. A personal search may yield additional sites, particularly since new Web pages are appearing on a daily basis.

Legal Links

One excellent source to begin your search for specialty areas is called Legal Links and is located at:

http://www.amicus.ca/resources/index.html

This site provides excellent information for paralegals looking for specific practice areas or background information on a law-related topic. Students or paralegals unfamiliar with the specialized practice area are wise to use this site for resources. It is also useful in those situations that require more than the normal federal and state links available at other sites. Practice areas included at this site are:

1. Civil litigation
2. Family law
3. Probate law

4. Real property law

5. Business, corporate, and securities law

6. Tax law

7. Personal injury

8. Health and disability

9. Bankruptcy

10. Insurance law

11. Constitutional law

12. Civil rights

13. Labor and employment law

14. Environmental law

Other non-law-related links provided on this page include information on the law of cyberspace, hardware and software, help with using the Internet, tips on searches and e-mail, and even assistance with Web site construction.

Law Around the Net

Another excellent source for beginning a search for legal resources, legal services, or attorneys by specialty area is the Law Around the Net site located at:

http://www.law.net/roundnet.phtml

This site provides a drop-down list from which you may begin your search. Their legal resources section provides access to courts, government offices, schools, and many other sources. The legal services area provides links to appraisers, bail bonding, court reporters, expert witnesses, paralegals, private investigation, and many others. A copy of their Web page is included as Figure 9-1 on page 93.

BANKRUPTCY

Title 11 of the United States Code contains the bankruptcy laws, which are federal statutes. It provides for a plan for debtors, who are unable to pay their creditors, to resolve those debts through dividing their assets

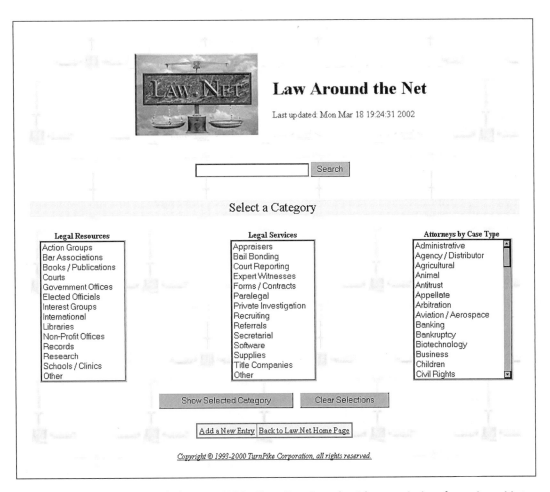

FIGURE 9-1 Law Around the Net Web Site. Reprinted with permission from **Law.Net**
© 1993–2000 TurnPike Corporation.

among the creditors. Some bankruptcy proceedings allow a debtor to stay
in business using income that is forthcoming to pay the debts. Bankruptcy
law allows debtors to discharge the financial obligations they have accu-
mulated, after their assets are distributed, even if their debts have not been
fully paid off.

Proceedings in bankruptcy are supervised and litigated in the United
States Bankruptcy Courts, which are a part of the Federal District Courts.
United States trustees handle the supervisory and administrative responsi-
bilities of the proceedings. These proceedings are governed by the
Bankruptcy Rules established by the United States Supreme Court.

The most common type of bankruptcy proceeding is a Chapter 7 (liquidation), which requires the appointment of a trustee who gathers the debtor's property that is not exempt, sells it, and pays the creditors from the proceeds. Chapter 11, 12, and 13 proceedings enable the debtor to develop a plan for paying his creditors over a period of time.

The official site for the Federal Judiciary home page is located at:

http://www.uscourts.gov/

By using "bankruptcy" as a key word search on this page, information about the bankruptcy courts may be obtained. Bankruptcy filings are also accessible from this page, as well as news about the bankruptcy courts. Links are provided to the bankruptcy courts in the various states as well.

As discussed earlier, the FindLaw site is an excellent source for many specialty areas of law, including bankruptcy. Again, this site is found at:

http://www.findlaw.com

The FindLaw Consumer Law Center provides information on bankruptcy law for consumers, an explanation of the various types of bankruptcy, links to bankruptcy courts, bankruptcy law information, and links to attorneys who specialize in bankruptcy law. There are also links to federal bankruptcy courts, which list their court decisions.

An Internet Bankruptcy Library is provided at:

http://bankrupt.com/

This site includes news, publications, resource materials, an online directory of bankruptcy clerks, consumer bankruptcy issues, and links to other bankruptcy resources.

CIVIL RIGHTS

Civil rights laws relate to the rights of citizens guaranteed by the United States Constitution, including freedom of speech, freedom of association, and freedom of religion. The civil rights amendments to the Constitution (the 13th, 14th, and 15th) deal with slavery, discrimination, and the right to vote, respectively. The Civil Rights Acts are federal laws relating to the prohibition of discrimination based on race, color, age, sex, religion, or national origin.

Attorneys who practice in this legal specialty area generally cialize in Constitutional Law. One of the major organizations in tl the American Civil Liberties Union (ACLU), which is a non nonprofit public-interest organization that is devoted to protect the rights of all individuals. Their Web page may be found at:

http://www.aclu.org/

A considerable amount of information is available on their Web page, including the following:

1. Information about the organization
2. Issues of church and state
3. Criminal justice issues
4. Death penalty information
5. Rights of immigrants
6. Gay rights
7. Women's rights
8. Racial equality
9. Voting rights
10. Lie detector testing
11. Drug testing and the work environment

A number of issues related to civil rights and liberties are also included in this Web page.

The civil rights provisions of the United States Code are available at:

http://www.cornell.edu/uscode/42/ch21.html

An extensive site that was established by the University of Minnesota Law School with database search capabilities provided by West Publishing, is located at:

http://www.umn.edu/humanrts/

This site focuses on important human rights–related international treaties, as well as other materials, with authoritative citations provided. Links are given for the Human Rights Commission, the Inter-American Court of Human Rights Organization on Security and Cooperation in Europe, the Resource Information Center, the INS Asylum Branch, and information about sessions of the United Nations Commission on Human Rights.

CONSUMER LAW

Several online libraries exist with information on consumer law. The following libraries provide links to a vast amount of information about the rights of consumers:

http://www.consumerlaw.org

http://www.consumerlawpage.com

The National Fraud Information Center in Washington, D.C. provides a Web site to allow consumers a method for reporting fraud. These reports are referred to the fraud database, administered by the Federal Trade Commission, the FBI, the Secret Service, the SEC, United States attorneys, and postal inspectors. This site is located at:

http://www.fraud.org/

INTELLECTUAL PROPERTY/COPYRIGHT LAW

Intellectual property and copyright laws are in a state of flux in relation to the Internet. Experts differ as to the extent the copyright laws cover the Internet itself in relation to copying material from Web pages. New laws will be developed in this area.

The United States Copyright Office maintains its own Web site at:

http://www.lcweb.loc.gov/copyright/

It contains an extensive amount of material on copyright law, including the law itself. Other items that may be found on this page include:

1. Speeches and press releases
2. Publications and information about the office itself
3. Copyright registration and application forms
4. Brochures on the copyright process
5. Conducting a search on copyright records
6. Links to other pages on copyright law
7. Federal regulations related to copyright law

The Copyright Clearance Center provides information about copyright licenses for a wide variety of copyright holders and may be found at:

http://www.copyright.com/

CORPORATE LAW

Corporate law is an area of business law that concerns the creation and dissolution of corporations. It includes tax law, dealings with the SEC, and preparation of corporate formation and dissolution documentation.

Information about large government contracts is provided at the Commerce Business Daily site. It lists abstracts of proposed contracts on a daily basis. This site is located at:

http://www.ld.com/cbd/

If a client of your firm were about to enter into a contract with a large government agency in a given subject area, it would be advantageous to do some research on this site to determine what other contracts have been provided.

A description of limited liability companies and how they operate may be found at:

http://www.roninsoft.com/llc.htm

or

http://www.4inc.com/llcfaq.htm

This site includes key documents used in the formation of these companies. Visit this site if a client is interested in forming a limited liability company.

A link for locating all state home pages for their secretaries of state is found at:

http://www.sos.state.il.us/govt/st_link.html

The office of the secretary of state for your state may provide the appropriate forms and documents for forming a corporation in that state. It will also provide information on how to form a corporation and the laws related to its formation.

A number of databases may be accessed via links provided on this page, including:

1. Nonprofit corporations
2. Charities databases
3. UCC
4. Trademarks
5. State government offices relating to corporations

Several states' Business and Professions Codes are available via links to the following site:

http://www.law.cornell.edu/topics/state_statutes.html

Dun and Bradstreet provides information on more than 60,000 companies with Web sites at:

http://www.companiesonline.com/

Blue Sky Laws (securities regulations) are available at:

http://www.seclaw.com/bluesky.htm

This site includes state orders regulating securities offerings on the Internet, Uniform Securities Act, state laws and cases, and links to federal securities agencies and federal law.

The complete Securities Act of 1933 may be found at:

http://www.speculativebubble.com/terms/sa1933.shtml

or at

http://www.techlawjournal.com/statutes/securities.asp

The Securities and Exchange Commission maintains its own site at:

http://www.sec.gov/

There is a considerable amount of information about the SEC itself on this site, as well as laws and regulations related to the transfer of shares of stock. Examine these sites if your firm's client is about to transfer shares of stock.

CRIMINAL LAW

The practice of criminal law involves the prosecution and defense of individuals accused of crimes. Prosecutors are generally district attorneys or prosecutors employed by the government. Defense attorneys may be either public defenders employed by the government or private attorneys. An excellent source for information about criminal law is the FindLaw site described and shown in Chapter 5.

The Institute for Law and Justice in Virginia provides links to criminal justice sites at:

http://www.ilj.org/

In addition to providing research and consulting services in criminal justice, this site provides links to government agencies and various criminal subspecialty areas such as substance abuse, corrections, sentencing, juvenile justice, courts, federal and state court decisions, and state and federal criminal codes. This represents a very inclusive page of links in the area of criminal law.

A site providing links to information about the criminal laws of Canada is located at:

http://www.brooksandmarshall.com/

Information on this site is useful to individuals facing criminal charges in Canada or to those who have a general interest in how the Canadian criminal legal process works. Detailed information is provided about the criminal process, including arrest, charge, bail, pleas, court, trial, jury, sentencing, appeals, pardons, and other related information.

Another page that provides a number of links to other pages in the criminal law area is located at:

http://www.payles.com/law/criminal.html

Included are sites about criminal justice, criminal defense, defense litigation, constitutions, statutes, codes, Supreme Court decisions, noteworthy criminal decisions, prison law, uniform crime reports, search and seizure issues, and sentencing.

ELDER LAW

Elder law actually encompasses many other specialty areas of law and is growing rapidly. Senior citizens are the largest and fastest-growing group in the United States. Along with becoming a senior citizen comes a whole range of legal problems and needs, ranging from health issues to estate planning. Included are issues of entitlement, Social Security, disability, Medicare, Medicaid, making of wills, probating estates, long-term care, and other special needs issues.

One Web site that provides many links to Web pages for elder law may be found at:

http://www.catalaw.com/topics/Elder/shtml

Links are provided to sites about health and welfare, disability, wills, trusts, and estates. National sites include elder care and senior law. Elder law links are also provided for Canada and Australia.

The Senior Law home page is located at:

http://www.seniorlaw.com

Information is provided about Medicare, elder law, Medicaid, estate planning, and the rights of the elderly. Links to court decisions, elder abuse statutes, estate planning, and other law resources are provided.

ENVIRONMENTAL LAW

The area of environmental law is one of the fastest growing in the United States today. Air and water pollution are of major concern in our large metropolitan areas. The federal government and state governments have established many environmental regulations for companies and individuals to save the environment.

One site that offers information about environmental issues all over the world is located at:

http://www.econet.apc.org/

It provides links to a number of resources in the Western Hemisphere, including North America, South America, and Central America. It also has links to sites pertaining to environmental law in Europe, Asia, and Africa. This site has been provided by the Environmental Law Alliance Worldwide through their United States office.

The Worldwide Web Virtual Library has a central site for many environmental law resources. This site is an excellent place to start a search of environmental law issues, and may be found at:

http://www.vlib.org/

The International Earth Science Information Network Consortium operates a data center for the National Aeronautics and Space Administration (NASA). Their site provides information from the World Conservation Union, the United Nations Environment Program, the World Resources Institute, and the British Columbia Ministry of Environment, Land, and Parks. The site includes many environmental treaties and agreements, including world treaties for the protection of the environment. It may be found at:

http://www.ciesin.org

A number of government agencies are devoted to the preservation of the environment, including the following, whose purposes are indicated along with their Web pages:

1. Environmental Protection Agency
   http://www.epa.gov/

   The EPA is located in Washington, D.C. and is an agency of the federal government. It is devoted to the study and regulation of environmental issues.

2. U.S. Geological Survey
   http://www.usgs.gov/

   This federal agency is devoted to geological issues, as well as mapping and water preservation.

3. Wetlands Regulation Center
   http://www.wetlands.com/

   This site, sponsored by the Environmental Technical Services Company in Austin, Texas, gives the provisions of the Clean Water Act for the preservation of wetlands and our waterways.

ESTATE PLANNING

Estate planning involves preparation of wills and other estate plans for clients, probate, and the preparation of trusts. Probate statutes for many states may be found at:

http://www.law.cornell.edu/topics/state_statutes.html

Use this site in an estate planning practice if the state law on a particular issue is in question.

A large collection of information about resources devoted to the area of trusts and estates may be found at the Web site for the United States House of Representatives links at:

http://www.house.gov/

FAMILY LAW

Family law includes all law that deals with families, including divorce, dissolution, child custody, child support, visitation, adoption, child welfare, and domestic violence. The most common area in law offices is divorce or dissolution. Family law is governed by state law; therefore, the researcher must find resources from the appropriate state.

An excellent site for information on divorce, property issues, child custody, and support is:

http://www.nolo.com/

Presented by Nolo Press, which is well known for publishing self-help books on many areas of law, this site provides discussion of custody agreements, divorce, tax planning, property issues, and many other issues that must be considered when obtaining a divorce. Although located in California, they also provide information on other states' laws.

A number of issues related to divorce are included at:

http://www.divorcenet.com/

Issues of cohabitation, custody, visitation, rights of grandparents, military divorce, paternity, and other related matters are discussed.

The World Wide Web Virtual Law Library provides a number of family law resources at:

http://www.law.indiana.edu/v-lib/

The statutes in the area of domestic relations are provided for a number of states at:

http://www.deltabravo.net/custody/statutes.htm

The United States Office of Child Support Enforcement provides information about this issue, as well as links to the states' sites at:

http://www.acf.dhhs.gov/programs/cse

A site that provides information about divorce laws in all 50 states may be found at:

http://www.divorcenet.com/

A number of links to issues related to domestic violence may be found at:

http://www.soros.org/crime/DVDir-Biblio.html

IMMIGRATION LAW

The Immigration and Naturalization Service (INS) is a federal agency that handles the admission, naturalization, and deportation of foreign nationals. (See the previous description in Chapter 6.) It is also responsible for the prevention of illegal entry of nonresident aliens. Its Web site may be found at:

http://www.ins.usdoj.gov/

The INS issues procedures and forms to be used in the immigration process. The American Immigration Center provides this information on their Web site at:

http://www.us-immigration.com

One may obtain tutorials, books, videos, software, and sample forms and kits to aid in the immigration process. Other material provided on the Web site includes:

1. Do-it-yourself immigration information
2. Documents on obtaining citizenship
3. Application preparation assistance
4. Immigration forms for downloading
5. Immigration attorney directory
6. Work visa information

The site for American Immigration Resources on the Net is located at:

http://www.wave.net/upg/immigration/resource.html

Information available from this site includes:

1. Links to United States immigration laws
2. Regulations and procedures
3. Immigration lawyers and organizations
4. Extensive links to related laws
5. Sampson bill
6. INS home page
7. State Department visa information
8. Immigration forms
9. Immigration Nationality and Citizenship Law
10. Case law
11. State Department immigration information
12. Foreign student immigration issues

The Immigration Superhighway page is a vast resource providing information and links to most relevant material in the immigration field. It is located at:

http://www.immigration-usa.com/is.html

Information on the following topics may be found there:

1. Immigration forum
2. Immigration and nationality act
3. Changing status and extending visits
4. Obtaining a green card
5. How to change status to permanent residence
6. Eligibility for visas
7. Foreign student immigration status
8. Diversity immigrant visa lottery
9. Cuban legal immigration program
10. American visas for investors and treaty traders
11. Immigration forms
12. Articles of current interest

A helpful site for immigrants wishing to assimilate into the American lifestyle is provided at:

http://www.lifeintheusa.com/

Helpful hints at this side provide:

1. Keys to understanding and adjusting to American life
2. Links to employment, business, public service, transportation, government, immigration, and citizenship

INTERNATIONAL LAW

International law involves both legal relationships and interactions between different countries, and legal relations between individuals or corporations from different countries. It also includes international trade agreements, treaties, and contracts. These sites are helpful if your client is doing business in a foreign country, doing business with a foreign corporation, or is itself a foreign corporation.

A number of foreign countries have their constitutions available online, including those listed below:

1. Latin America countries (in Spanish)
   http://161.132.29.12/CCD/constitucion/constitucion.html
2. Australia, most European countries, Canada, and Mexico
   http://www.ukans.edu/carrie/docs/docscon.html
3. Worldwide constitutions (many countries)
   http://www.eur.nl/iacl/const.html
4. Many countries' constitutions along with other material on constitutional law in these countries
   http://www.law.cornell.edu/law/index.html

Many countries have their laws, trade agreements, and treaties online, along with links to branches of their governments. Included in this list are the following:

1. British Parliament
   http://www.hmsoinfo.gov.uk/hmso/document/Acts.htm
2. Australia
   http://austlii.law.uts.edu.au/
3. Japan
   http://home.highway.or.jp/JAPANLAW/index.htm
4. Canada
   a. Copyright
      http://cancopy.com
   b. Legal links
      http://www.law.ubc.ca/links/bowers/bowers.html
   c. Law sources
      http://gahtan.com/lawlinks/
5. France
   http://www.fdn.fr/~rabenou/index.html

The Library of Congress maintains a site for the Global Legal Information Network and provides a database of laws from countries all over the world. It is often the best place to start when doing research into international law and is available at:

http://lcweb2.loc.gov/law/GLINv1/

The World Court maintains a Web site at:

http://www.lawschool.cornell.edu/lawlibrary/cijwww

and at

http://www.icj-cij.org/

This court, also known as the International Court of Justice, is the supreme judicial body of the United Nations. It handles controversies between nations, such as those involving fishing rights in international waters. The following materials are available on this site:

1. Statutes

2. Treaties

3. Decisions

4. Advisory opinions

5. United Nations charter

6. News about the United Nations

7. Student resources

8. International law Web sites

LITIGATION/PERSONAL INJURY LAW

Since the laws related to civil litigation are primarily state laws, see Chapter 7, which covers the methods of finding the laws for your state. For the federal laws, see Chapter 6, which discusses federal law. Some specialized sites for managing cases in civil litigation and personal injury will be provided here and may be used for state or federal cases.

Sometimes these suits involve defendants who are large corporations. Hoovers Online compiles data on public companies including history and financial conditions. Hoovers may be found at:

http://www.hoovers.com

Conducting an investigation into locating people and their public records is another aspect of civil litigation. In addition to the Web sites discussed earlier, specific sources available for this purpose include the following:

1. People and businesses
   http://www.databaseamerica.com
   http://www.people.yahoo.com/
   http://www.switchboard.com

2. Motor vehicle records
   http://www.knowx.com   (fee-based)
   For a nominal fee, public records and motor vehicle in
   are available.

3. Links to motor vehicle records
   http://www.inil.com/users/dguss/wgator.htm

Cases against automobile manufacturers for defective products represent another specialty within personal injury law. The National Highway Traffic Safety Administration (NHTSA) maintains its own site providing data on traffic safety, vehicle problems, and consumer complaints. It may be accessed at:

http://www.nhtsa.dot.gov

Included in this site are links to other databases, including:

1. Technical Services Bulletins

   Automobile manufacturers provide bulletins to repair facilities about repair problems reported by vehicle owners and how to correct them.

2. Consumer Complaints

   A database of all complaints by consumers is provided here. Trends of particular problems with passenger cars and trucks are noted.

3. Recalls

   A separate database is maintained for those vehicles that have been recalled. Owners are notified of recalls that affect vehicle safety.

4. Investigations

   The National Highway Traffic Safety Administration initiates its own investigations after many consumers have complained about the same problem with an automobile. Results of these investigations are available. Before doing research on this site, be sure to note the model, make, year, and suspected problem with the vehicle.

Similar data for other consumer products is available at the Consumer Product Safety Commission's site at:

http://www.cpsc.gov

Descriptions of products that have been recalled is provided, as well as press releases and other information valuable to consumers. If your practice is primarily involved with products liability actions, then you may wish to subscribe to the Consumer Product Safety Commission's listserv. You will be sent (via e-mail) safety information and product recalls. To subscribe to this service, send the following e-mail message:

TO: **listproc@cpsc.gov**
FROM: <your screen name>
BODY: sub CPSCINFO-L <your screen name>

Another aspect of the civil litigation process in personal injury law is reading medical records and calculating damages. The value of a suit is directly related to an understanding of the extent of medical injuries incurred by the plaintiff. A thorough understanding of reading medical records assists in this process. An excellent site for this purpose is located at the Virtual Medical Center at:

http://www.mediconsult.com

Links on this site give categories for injuries.

If information is needed on the effects of certain prescription drugs, the following link is available:

http://www.rxlist.com

Expert Witnesses

Most cases involving personal injuries require expert witnesses. In addition to the usual medical experts, any number of others may be required. Sites that provide links to experts of all kinds are available at:

http://www.expertpages.com

http://www.hgexperts.com

Also available are links to court reporters, private investigators, and process servers.

A fee-based service that will provide transcripts of prior expert witness testimony is available at:

http://www.trialsdigest.com/research/

Defense attorneys may also obtain information about expert witnesses from a site of over 2,000 firms who share information on experts, articles they have written, and their prior testimony, at:

http://www.idex.com

Damages

One of the most important aspects of the civil suit is the assessment and evaluation of damages. The Internet provides sites that show data from lawsuits that have been previously settled. Two of these sites are located at:

http://www.lweekly.com

http://www.ljextra.com/cgi-bin/vds

The Kelley Blue Book site provides data on the value of automobiles and is located at:

http://www.kbb.com

REAL PROPERTY LAW

The area of real property law involves a number of different specialties, including real estate sales, litigation over real estate transactions, and landlord/tenant issues. In some states, real estate sales transactions utilize escrow companies to complete the sale; in others law firms complete this process in what is known as a "closing." Paralegals may assist in all of these areas.

Real Estate Transactions

The Real Estate Transaction Network provides a method for conducting real estate transactions online. Their Data Track Systems offer links with real estate companies, mortgage providers, title companies, and real estate appraisers enabling a rapid transfer of information for real estate sales. Their site is located at:

http://www.realtycheck.com

A similar site is at

http://www.rexnetwork.com

The National Association of Realtors maintains its own site at:

http://www.commercialsource.com

or at

http://www.realtor.com

In addition to providing over 400,000 listings of property for sale in most states, it also offers links to information concerning the value of real estate.

A link for those interested in international properties is provided.

The California Association of Realtors has developed a particularly noteworthy site at:

http://www.car.org

This site provides the largest source listing of California properties on the Internet. It also has links to continuing education and professional development in real estate, legislative information, news, research, economics, legal resources online for real estate matters, and many other helpful links.

For individuals involved in the commercial real estate market, the Commercial Real Estate Network is maintained by the Certified Commercial Investment Members (CCIM) organization, which is dedicated to facilitating networking and information sharing between its members and the general public. CCIM is a professional organization for those in commercial real estate brokerage, asset management, valuation, investment analysis, and leasing. The site provides market trends in commercial real estate, discussion forums, links to other Internet sites, and a calendar of events of the organization. The site is located at:

http://www.ccim.com

A listing of real estate appraisers by state may be found at:

http://www.inrealty.com/

This site also provides resources related to appraisals, accounting, brokerage, demographics, economics, finance, insurance, taxation, law, and management.

Information on state licensing requirements as well as how to contact various states' real estate commissions and regulatory agencies is located at:

http://www.real-estate-ed.com/docs/usmap.htm

Landlord/Tenant Issues

Nolo Press, a self-help legal book publisher in Cali[f]
of articles on landlord/tenant law, and on issues i[n]
homeowners, neighborhoods, and safety, at:

http://www.nolo.com/home.htm

Additional information about landlord/tenant law is available on individual lawyers' home pages. It is important to always determine when the page was last updated to be sure to obtain the latest laws and rulings.

TAX LAW

Attorneys who practice in tax law must be familiar with the tax laws of the federal government as well as of their individual states. The federal regulations on taxes are available on the following sites:

1. Virtual Law Library
   http://www.law.indiana.edu/law/v-lib.taxes.html

   This site provides several links to a number of different sources in tax law.

2. Internal Revenue Service
   http://www.irs.ustreas.gov/

   The IRS site provides information about where to file taxes, how to get assistance, tax forms, and instructions for forms completion.

3. United States Tax Code
   http://www.law.cornell.edu/uscode/26/
   http://www.tns.lcs.mit.edu/uscode/ (key word searches)

A few sites provide information on both state and federal tax regulations. Among the more comprehensive sites is:

http://www.best.com:80/%/7Eftmexpat/html/taxsites.html

In addition to providing documents and forms for federal taxes, this site provides links to news groups, tax articles, legislative and judicial resources, tax treaties, state tax laws, social security, and foreign taxes.

One site that provides a number of links to both federal and state tax law sites is located at:

http://www.el.com/elinks/Taxes/

SUMMARY

Many specialty areas of law are discussed in this chapter. A large number of links in each specialty area are provided. Sources that provided information in several practice areas are also given.

REVIEW QUESTIONS

1. What is the Web address of the bankruptcy court closest to your home?
2. What is the Web address of the secretary of state's office in your state?
3. Does your state have a state income tax? If so, list the Web page for your state's tax laws.
4. What is the major federal environmental agency? List its Web site.
5. Name a major organization in the area of constitutional law and list its Web page.

PRACTICAL PROBLEMS

1. The attorney has asked you to investigate the legality of lie detector testing as it relates to civil rights. Prepare a memorandum reporting your findings.
2. A client is suing the builder of his new home for construction defects related to improper pouring of the cement that caused the concrete foundation and his floor tile to crack after only six months of use. Find an expert on this type of defect in your geographical area. Write a memorandum to the attorney identifying the expert and discussing his or her area of expertise and qualifications.

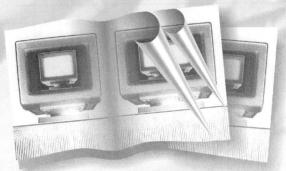

CHAPTER 10

Westlaw

INTRODUCTION

The Westlaw computer-assisted legal research (CALR) systems enable you to access current information at any time and in any place. You can search thousands of legal records and documents and read case material almost immediately after the court has handed down the decision. With access as simple as obtaining an account, getting online, and finding the Westlaw Web page, these systems have become easier to use than ever before. In a matter of minutes you are connected to the Westlaw system. Prior to putting research materials online, editors check them for accuracy and add parallel citations, editorial comments, and descriptions. Westlaw is linked to the West books and CD-ROM library through the West key numbering system.

Twenty-four-hour access is provided to the Westlaw research materials online. Entry is provided to thousands of different databases, representing billions of pages of information.

THE NEW WESTLAW

A new system has been devised whereby Web technology has been combined with the more familiar book research to provide a consolidated and simple source of information. Tabs are furnished to view citations, tables of contents, statutes outlines, and other information without leaving the original document. The images on your screen are similar to a book's pages.

The system provides a research trail of all steps used in your current search so that you are able to navigate quickly through pages. Multiple databases can be searched simultaneously. A centralized source for key numbers assists in searches based on the West key numbering system.

SUBSCRIPTION INFORMATION

Westlaw

The easiest method of accessing Westlaw is through your Internet browser via the World Wide Web by using **http://www.westlaw.com**. You must first obtain an account from West, along with a password. You can then go to the Web page, key in your account number (client identifier) and password, and you are online with Westlaw.

Alternatively, you may obtain an account that includes Westmate software and connect to the database directly via your modem. You will need to load the software onto your computer and make use of special commands that are provided in the subscription materials.

Information about either of these two systems can be obtained through West's Customer Service Department at 1-800-Westlaw or 1-800-937-8529. Ordering and pricing information is available from West Sales Support at 1-800-328-9352.

CONDUCTING SEARCHES

Word Searches

A root expander is used for searching for specific words and their derivatives. If a word exists in several forms, the "!" symbol is used to find all forms of the word. For example, Westlaw may be instructed to find all forms of the word "give" by entering "giv!" into your query. In this way, you will find all occurrences of "give," "given," "giving," and all other words that begin with "giv."

Westlaw searches for the regular and irregular plural forms of the word automatically when you enter the singular form. Therefore, it is not necessary to use the "!" symbol if only the singular, plural, or possessive form of the word is required. If you wish to search only for the exact word and not its plural form, limit the search with a "#" entered before the word itself. For example, "#give" will allow a search for only the word "give."

The universal character symbol "*" operates as if you were using it to search for material on your hard drive or a diskette. This sign represents any character of the alphabet. Using more than one sign enables a search for more than one character. This symbol must be used with care, however, since some searches will reveal words that are not at all related to your search. For example, using "f*ll" in your search would yield "fall," "fell," "full," and "fill." If you are searching for information for a personal injury "slip and fall" case, then you should write out the words "fall" and "fell" in your search query rather than using the "*" symbol. By using this method, you can ensure that only applicable material is found.

GETTING ONLINE WITH WESTLAW

In order to go immediately to Westlaw, perform the following steps on your computer:

1. Get on line with your Web browser, such as America Online, Netscape Navigator 3.0 or higher, or Microsoft Explorer 3.0 or higher.

2. In the "Go to" section of the page, key in the following address:

http://www.westlaw.com

and hit "enter."

3. Go to the "Sign on to westlaw.com" dialog box.

4. Type in your Westlaw password in the "Password" box and your client identifier in the Client ID box.

5. Click the "Sign on" button.

6. The "Welcome to westlaw.com" page will appear, and you are ready to start your research session.

If you choose to save your Westlaw password so that you don't have to key it each time you sign on, select the option on the sign-on screen that says "save this password." Note that anyone who uses your Web browser will be able to sign on to Westlaw with your saved password if you select this option. Therefore, it is advisable to use the option only when access to your computer is password protected.

If you wish to use the secure sign-on site feature, click this option so that your password will be encrypted as it is sent through the Internet.

Suppose, however, that you do not wish to go directly to this page. You may use the home page for law schools by substituting the following address for the one used in step 2 above:

http://lawschool.westlaw.com

This will enable you to access the home page for law schools where you may also find KeyCite, West's Educational Network (TWEN), the *West Legal Directory,* and Westlaw.

CREATING INTERNAL WEB SITES

One major advantage of using Westlaw online is the ability to set up internal Web sites to link content. Most legal offices have their own intranets that link members of the firm via their computers. Individuals in the office may conduct their research using Westlaw, file it in the firm's research files on their computer, and link the research so that it goes directly to a page on

http://www.westlaw.com

If someone else in the office is interested in the topic of that particular research, he or she may click the hyperlink and find the correct page.

By the use of *WestCiteLink,* a hyperlink can be created that links the citations in a document and the text of the case on Westlaw. Thus, if another member of the firm is conducting research into a given topic, that person may follow the existing link to the citations and cases.

KEYCITE

You are probably familiar with the system for updating cases and statutes in books. You must look through several citators to determine whether the case you wish to utilize has been overruled or amended before using it in your current document. Often several books have to be checked for the appropriate citation. This process may take several hours if many cases or statutes are being cited.

With the use of KeyCite, you may obtain this information by a click of the mouse on your computer. Information that might take several hours using books is acquired in minutes. The details of the case history are provided online within a few hours of the time the court opinion is received by West.

PRIMARY SOURCES

Primary sources, including cases and statutes for all 50 states and the District of Columbia, as well as the federal sources, are available on Westlaw. It is a relatively simple process to find cases from any of these places on any given subject by doing a "key word search" with all the words that must be present in the case. Within seconds the citations for the most recent cases are given on the screen. You merely click on the case in which you are interested, and that case appears on your screen.

Opinions of the United States Supreme Court are available within an hour of the time they are released by the court. The special "highlights" databases provide significant new court opinions on given topics on a daily basis.

Statutes from all the states as well as the federal system are available under the codes for the individual states, the federal codes, and the United States codes.

SECONDARY SOURCES

Almost any secondary source available in a library can be found on Westlaw. More than 10,000 databases can be accessed. Among these are legal newspapers, public records, international newspapers, general-interest magazines and journals, newsletters and trade publications on many topics, and press releases. Practice area materials are available in several different specialties, such as administrative law, bankruptcy, business organizations, government, family law, and many more. General texts and periodicals can be found, as well as treatises, practice guides, journals, and law reviews. The *West Legal Directory* provides information about attorneys throughout the United States and in some foreign countries.

BEGINNING YOUR RESEARCH SESSION

Figure 10-1 on page 118 represents the first page you will see when signing on to Westlaw. On the left side of the screen, you will see the "Begin Research" frame with four different choices:

1. Find a document by citation

   The first box enables you to find a document if you have the citation. Type the citation in the box and click the "Go" button. You will be taken to the document.

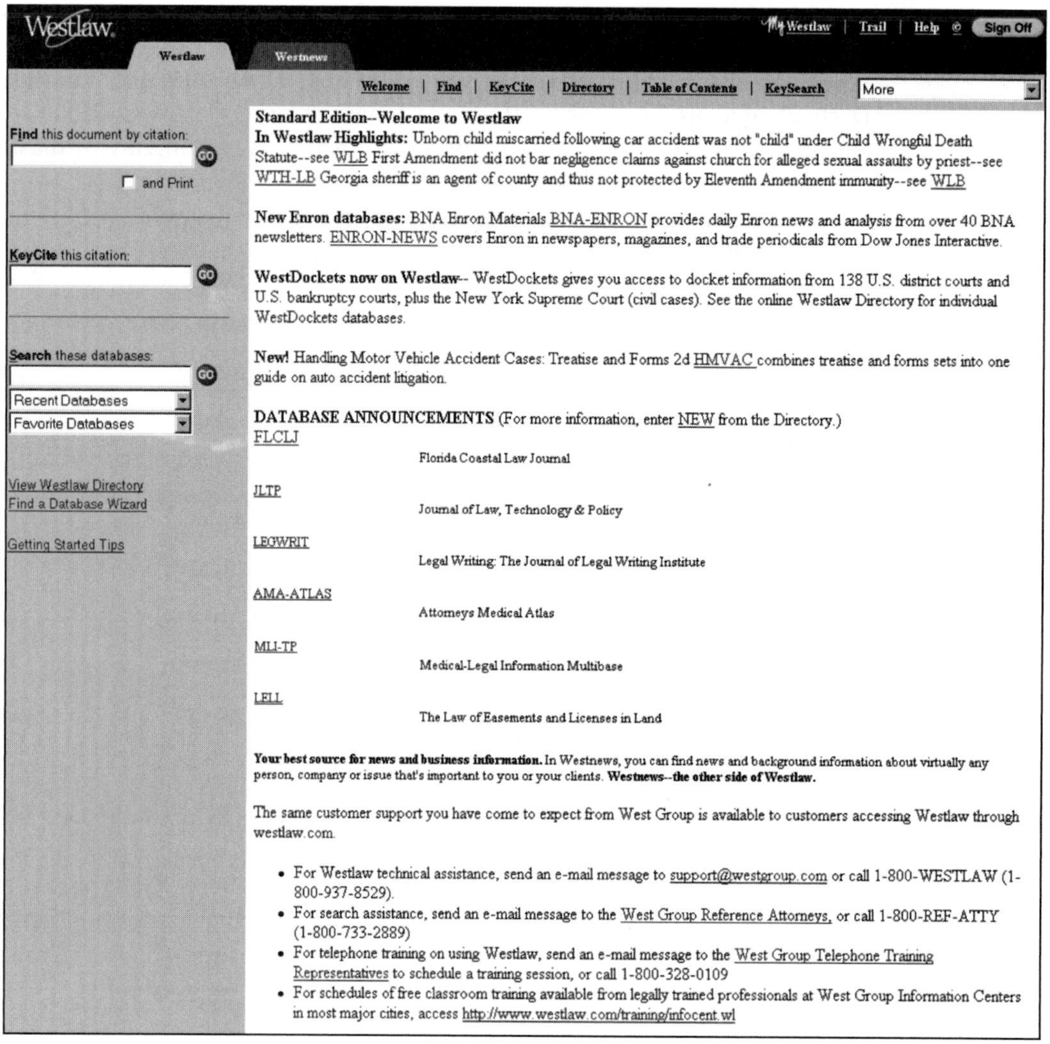

Westlaw.

Westlaw | Westnews

My Westlaw | Trail | Help | Sign Off

Welcome | Find | KeyCite | Directory | Table of Contents | KeySearch | More

Find this document by citation:

GO

and Print

KeyCite this citation:

GO

Search these databases:

GO

Recent Databases

Favorite Databases

View Westlaw Directory

Find a Database Wizard

Getting Started Tips

Standard Edition--Welcome to Westlaw

In Westlaw Highlights: Unborn child miscarried following car accident was not "child" under Child Wrongful Death Statute--see WLB First Amendment did not bar negligence claims against church for alleged sexual assaults by priest--see WTH-LB Georgia sheriff is an agent of county and thus not protected by Eleventh Amendment immunity--see WLB

New Enron databases: BNA Enron Materials BNA-ENRON provides daily Enron news and analysis from over 40 BNA newsletters. ENRON-NEWS covers Enron in newspapers, magazines, and trade periodicals from Dow Jones Interactive.

WestDockets now on Westlaw-- WestDockets gives you access to docket information from 138 U.S. district courts and U.S. bankruptcy courts, plus the New York Supreme Court (civil cases). See the online Westlaw Directory for individual WestDockets databases.

New! Handling Motor Vehicle Accident Cases: Treatise and Forms 2d HMVAC combines treatise and forms sets into one guide on auto accident litigation.

DATABASE ANNOUNCEMENTS (For more information, enter NEW from the Directory.)

FLCLJ
Florida Coastal Law Journal

JLTP
Journal of Law, Technology & Policy

LEGWRIT
Legal Writing: The Journal of Legal Writing Institute

AMA-ATLAS
Attorneys Medical Atlas

MLI-TP
Medical-Legal Information Multibase

LELL
The Law of Easements and Licenses in Land

Your best source for news and business information. In Westnews, you can find news and background information about virtually any person, company or issue that's important to you or your clients. **Westnews--the other side of Westlaw.**

The same customer support you have come to expect from West Group is available to customers accessing Westlaw through westlaw.com.

- For Westlaw technical assistance, send an e-mail message to support@westgroup.com or call 1-800-WESTLAW (1-800-937-8529).
- For search assistance, send an e-mail message to the West Group Reference Attorneys, or call 1-800-REF-ATTY (1-800-733-2889)
- For telephone training on using Westlaw, send an e-mail message to the West Group Telephone Training Representatives to schedule a training session, or call 1-800-328-0109
- For schedules of free classroom training available from legally trained professionals at West Group Information Centers in most major cities, access http://www.westlaw.com/training/infocent.wl

FIGURE 10-1 Westlaw Opening Page. Reprinted with permission from the Westlaw Web Page © 2002 West Group.

2. Check a citation

   If you want to check a citation for accuracy or updating, you may key it into the box for KeyCite.

3. Search these databases

   If you know the identifier for the database you wish to access, type it in this box and click the "Go" button. You will be taken to

the appropriate database. Note that a list of databases avail
on Westlaw is provided with subscription materials. Most of the
identifiers are relatively easy to remember. Among the most
common are:

Name of Item	Database Identifier
Federal case law	ALLFEDS
State case law (all states)	ALLSTATES
California cases*	CA-CS
New York cases*	NY-CS
Virginia Statutes Annotated*	VA-ST-ANN
Harvard Law Review	HVLR
Wall Street Journal	WSJ

4. Select a recent or favorite database

The last box on the left enables you to find the identifier for a
database. By using this drop-down list, you may access the database directory, the IDEN database that enables you to search for a
database, or the most commonly used Westlaw databases. You may
also access "Find" to retrieve a document by using its citation from
the "Select a database" drop-down list.

The top right side of the page has a drop-down list from which you may
choose different functions. By choosing the *Database Wizard,* you may access the Main Directory List of databases. This feature is useful if you are
not certain which database to access or if you know the name of the database but do not know its identifier. You can browse through sections of the
directory by clicking on the main icon for that directory. By clicking on
the icon of the database you wish to view, you may descend through
various sections of the database directories.

When browsing through the directory, notice the icon (I) to the left of
the name. Clicking on this icon will give you information about what is included in that database. The identifier for the particular database is found
in the right column of the list. The Database Directory page is shown in
Figure 10-2 on page 120.

When you cannot find the appropriate database, use the search feature
as follows:

1. On the left side of the Database Directory page, at the bottom of the
page, click the "Go" button under the "Search for Database" section.

---

* Use the state postal abbreviation for any state.

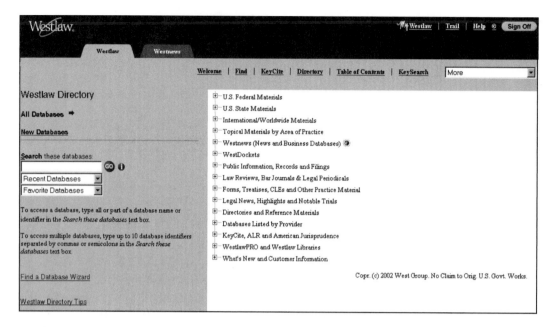

FIGURE 10-2 Westlaw Database Directory. Reprinted with permission from the *Westlaw Database Directory* © 2002 West Group.

2. You will see a text box on the right side that enables you to search for a database using Natural Language. Type a description of the database or the type of material in which you are interested.

3. Click the "Search" button.

4. Once you have completed your search, then click the "View Result" button.

5. You will see a list of databases that correspond to your description.

6. Click on the database identifier in which you are interested.

7. If you would like a description of the database, click the retrieval number of that database.

8. For a more detailed description of the database, click on the Scope icon (I) or the Scope option on the left side of the Search page.

9. To leave this function, click your browser's "Back" button.

Figure 10-3 shows the Main Directory List for the Westlaw Database Directory. Click the icon in front of the material if you wish to view the sections included in that particular directory. When you find the section in which you are interested, double-click on the name or identifier.

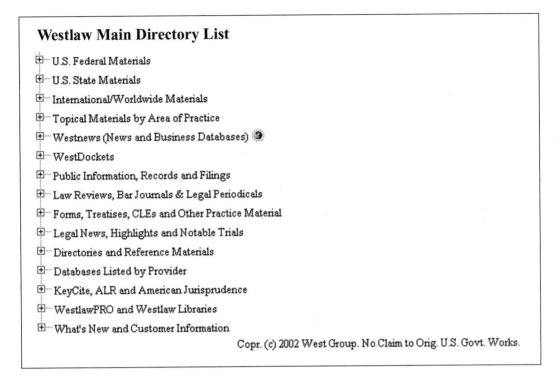

Copr. (c) 2002 West Group. No Claim to Orig. U.S. Govt. Works.

FIGURE 10-3 Westlaw Main Database Directory. Reprinted with permission from the Westlaw *Database Directory List* © 2002 West Group.

SPECIALIZED SEARCHES

If you are looking for a document and know its citation or title, you do not have to access a database. If you do not have either of these, you can still search by date or by issue. You can use the "Find" function or the Natural Language function (WIN) or conduct a search using "Terms & Connectors."

Finding a Document by Citation

Go back to the home page that says "Welcome to westlaw.com." Complete the following steps for finding a document by its citation number:

1. On the left side you will see a text box that says "Find this document by citation."
2. Type the citation for your document in the text box.

3. Click "Go."

If you are not at the "Welcome" page but are elsewhere in the Westlaw system, follow these steps:

1. Locate the drop-down list at the top of the page.
2. Select "Find a document."
3. Click "Go."
4. When the "Find a document" page appears, type the citation in the "Enter a citation" box on the left side of the screen.
5. Click "Go."

In most cases, punctuation and spacing are optional. However, your citation request must use the proper format for citations. Some examples of "Find" requests are indicated below:

Type of Document	*Citation Number Sample*
United States Code Annotated	22 USCA s 333 (or 22 usca s 333)
Federal Case	55 F2D 2222 (or 55 f2d 2222)

Finding a Document Using "Find"

Many publications are accessible by using the "Find" function. Notice the "Publications list" on the left side of the "Find" page. Click on this list to see all publications available using find. The abbreviations for these documents will also be included.

A copy of the "Find" page is shown in Figure 10-4. Note that the "Scan" feature enables you to search the list for key words or phrases.

Finding a Document by Title

Suppose you have the name of a document but do not know the citation number. You can restrict your search by using the title field and the name of your document. First you must access the appropriate database. For example, if you were seeking the case of *Miller v. California* and you knew it was a United States Supreme Court case, you would search the database for the Supreme Court (SCT). Type the following inquiry in the "Terms & Connectors Query" text box and click "Search":

ti(miller & california)

In order to see the case, click the "View result" field.

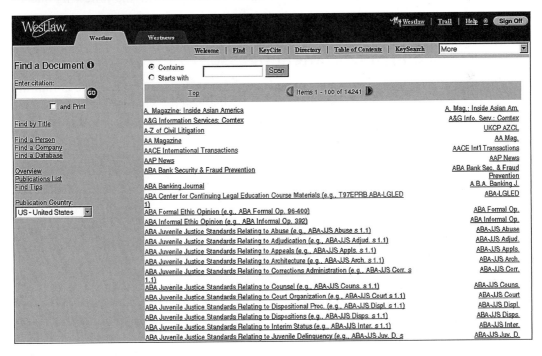

FIGURE 10-4   Westlaw Find Page. Reprinted with permission from the Westlaw Find
Page © 2002 West Group.

To perform a search by title, you must precede the name of the document by the term "ti". Instead of using "v." in a case name, you must use "&". Capitalization is not required, and general terms such as plaintiff, defendant, company, or corporation should be excluded. Unique terms from the title should be used if the case name is long. For example, if you were searching for a case called *Jonathan Danielli Enterprises, Inc. v. Michael Jeffries Manufacturing Company, Inc.*, you would use the following search term:

ti(Danielli & Jeffries)

To find a case where both the plaintiff and the defendant have the same name, you must use the **"+p"** connector. For example, to find the California case of *Marvin v. Marvin,* type the following query:

ti(marvin +p marvin)

While case name titles use the names of the parties, law reviews or other periodicals use the exact title of the article itself. For example, to find an article entitled "Surrogate Parenting" in the *Harvard Law Review,* search by title in the database for *Harvard Law Review* with the following query:

ti(surrogate parenting)

Finding a Document by Issue

The most critical aspect of searching for a document by its issue is framing the issue itself. You must also determine exactly what types of documents you wish to retrieve. Often other resources are valuable for this preliminary investigation, including digests, treatises, legal encyclopedias, periodicals, and hornbooks.

Once you have read these materials, you may be ready to frame your issue. Make a list of all pertinent terminology, facts, and concepts that define your research. From these key words, write an issue in one or two sentences. For instance, you may have an issue that states:

May an owner of real property transfer ownership and still maintain a homestead?

After you have written the issue, determine what other words have the same meaning and might be used in any documents you are searching. For instance, in the example issue, "real property" can also be referred to as "real estate."

Next, you must decide what types of documents you wish to retrieve as well as where you can find them on Westlaw. Ask yourself the following questions:

1. What type of case do I have?
2. In what jurisdiction is the case being heard?

Your list of databases should be consulted to determine the appropriate choices. For instance, if you wish to search all jurisdictions, then you would use the ALLCASES database. However, if you are searching only New York cases, you would use the New York cases database. A checklist has been provided in Figure 10-5 to assist in the search steps.

1. **Preliminary research documents**
   A. Encyclopedia
   B. Hornbook
   C. Treatise
   D. Other
2. **Frame the issue**
   Issue statement: _____
   A. All key words _____
   B. Thesaurus terms _____
3. **What documents do I want?** _____
   _____
4. **Natural language or terms and connectors?** _____
   _____
5. **List of databases to search:**
   Federal _____
   All states _____
   State of _____ only _____
   Others: _____   _____
   _____   _____
   _____   _____

FIGURE 10-5 Checklist for Searching by Issue in Westlaw

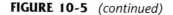

6. Have I found all relevant materials? _____

   _____

7. Do I want to expand my search to other databases or
   sources? _____

   _____

FIGURE 10-5 *(continued)*

Now that you have all of the preliminary information, you are ready to begin your search using the Natural Language feature of Westlaw called WIN or "Westlaw Is Natural." The steps to follow are given in Figure 10-6.

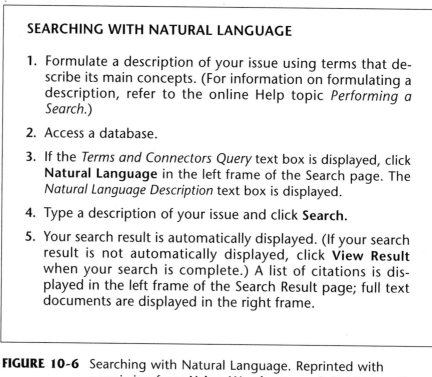

SEARCHING WITH NATURAL LANGUAGE

1. Formulate a description of your issue using terms that describe its main concepts. (For information on formulating a description, refer to the online Help topic *Performing a Search*.)

2. Access a database.

3. If the *Terms and Connectors Query* text box is displayed, click **Natural Language** in the left frame of the Search page. The *Natural Language Description* text box is displayed.

4. Type a description of your issue and click **Search**.

5. Your search result is automatically displayed. (If your search result is not automatically displayed, click **View Result** when your search is complete.) A list of citations is displayed in the left frame of the Search Result page; full text documents are displayed in the right frame.

FIGURE 10-6 Searching with Natural Language. Reprinted with permission from **Using Westlaw.com** © 2002 West Group.

Refining Tools

Several devices are available on Westlaw to further refine your search. These tools help to make your search easier and more comprehensive.

If you wish to have certain phrases appear in your description of the issue and in the search results, you may enclose them in quotation marks. For instance, to have the phrase "res ipsa loquitur" appear in your search result, type it in quotation marks in your issue phrase.

You may wish to have related concepts added to your description. Westlaw provides an online thesaurus to assist in this endeavor. Once you have typed your issue statement into the text box, click "Thesaurus." Look through the "Terms in the Description" list and select that term for which you want to use related concepts. Click "View Related Terms." Select the concept you wish to add to your issue and click "Add Term(s) to Description." Once you complete this process, click "Go" and then the "Search" button to begin your search.

If you cannot find the related term for which you are searching in the Westlaw thesaurus, you may add it by typing the description in parentheses immediately following the concept to which it relates in your issue statement.

You may further refine your search by using Control Concepts, which allows you to specify terms that must appear in every document in your result. Type your explanation in the "Natural Language Description" box and click "Control Concepts." When the Concepts list appears on the right side of the page, select the concept you wish to appear in every document and click "Go."

Searching by Terms & Connectors

In some cases, you may not want to use the Natural Language search feature of Westlaw. Instead you may want to conduct a search by using "Terms & Connectors" in the following manner:

1. Formulate all of the terms you wish to use in your search. Alternatives will be discussed in the section following this list.

2. Determine the specific connectors you wish to use between the search terms.

3. Access the database you need for this particular search.

4. Select the "Terms & Connectors" search method.

5. Enter your issue.

Terminology for Terms & Connectors Searches

A search using the "Terms & Connectors" method is somewhat different from a "Natural Language" search. Consider the following when writing your issue:

1. *Alternative words*—Use synonyms and antonyms, variations of terms. For example, if your search involved the word "litigation," you would also want to use the term "lawsuit." You can check the Westlaw thesaurus for alternative terms to use in your query.

2. *Common words*—Avoid common words. If the term you enter is too common, you will receive a message that your terms are too common to be searched. An exception is the use of a hyphenated term as either the first or last word of your query.

3. *Plurals/possessives*—Westlaw will automatically retrieve all plural forms of words used in your issue. However, it will not retrieve the singular form if you enter the plural. The same holds true for the use of possessive terms. If you enter the word without the possessive, Westlaw will retrieve both the nonpossessive and possessive forms of the word. However, if you enter only the possessive form, the nonpossessive form will not be retrieved.

4. *Acronyms*—In order to retrieve all forms of the acronym, enter the name with periods and no spaces, and spell out the words that make up the acronym as well. For example, to find information about General Motors Corporation, you would use the following terms in your search:

    "GM"

    "General Motors"

5. *Root Expanders*—In order to retrieve all forms of a word, you must use the "!" root expander. In other words, if you wish to find all forms of the word "sleep," you would enter the following term:

    "sleep!"

    and would retrieve the following variations of the word:

    sleeping

    sleeps

    sleeper

6. *Asterisk*—The asterisk is used to take the place of a variable character. Use as many asterisks as you wish to show that number of variable characters. For example, using

   dr*nk

   will yield "drink," "drank," or "drunk."

7. *Connectors*—Rules for using connectors follow:

   a. Either/or

   A space between words indicates at least one of the terms must appear in the document.

   b. All terms (&)

   The & sign retrieves documents containing two or more of the search terms; however, they may be contained anywhere in the document.

   c. Same sentence (/s) or paragraph (/p)

   Using the /p connector requires that the same terms must appear in the same paragraph. Using the /s requires that the same terms must appear in the same sentence.

   d. Certain number of words (/n)

   Using a numerical connector will require that the same terms must appear within that number of words (n represents a number).

   e. Terms in quotation marks (" ")

   Terms must appear in the same order as they appear within the quotation marks.

   f. Excluding terms with %

   Search terms following the % symbol should be excluded from the search.

Some examples of the preceding rules follow:

- **Attorney malpractice doctor** will retrieve any documents that contain any one of those terms.
- **Attorney & malpractice & doctor** will retrieve documents containing all three terms anywhere in the document.
- **Attorney /p malpractice /p doctor** will retrieve documents containing all three terms within the same paragraph.

- **Attorney /s malpractice /s doctor** will retrieve documents containing all three terms within the same sentence.
- **Attorney /5 malpractice** will retrieve documents containing the word "attorney" within five words of the word "malpractice."

Although the Terms & Connectors search may appear to be more difficult and cumbersome than the Natural Language search, there will often be situations where the use of the code terms applicable in this type of search are more beneficial for finding appropriate documents for your issue statement. Additional terms will allow you to restrict your search by date or by court.

Finding Documents by Date

If you are searching for cases, statutes, or articles published on a certain date or within a range of dates, go to the Terms & Connectors search page and perform the following steps:

1. Click "Field Restrictions" on the Terms & Connectors search page.
2. Choose "Data DA" from the list.
3. Type the date within parentheses.
4. Click "Go."

See Figure 10-7 for a picture of the Terms & Connectors search page.
An alternative method for finding a document by date follows:

1. Type **"da"** in the Terms & Connectors query text box.
2. Type the date or date range in parentheses, being sure to type the year with four digits, e.g., 1988.

Some acceptable formats for dates follow:

da 9-6-1977	for documents dated September 6, 1977
da(bef 1977)	for documents before 1977
da (bef 10-10-2000)	for documents before October 10, 2000
da (aft 1979 and bef 1985)	for documents 1980–1984

SURVEYING RETRIEVED DOCUMENTS————————

Various methods are provided to browse the documents you have retrieved to determine if they are applicable to your original issue statement. Westlaw furnishes procedures for surveying retrieved documents, changing the display, and moving between documents on your screen.

Note the search result page on the display. On the left side, you will see a list of citations applicable to your issue statement. The right side comprises the actual text of the documents from the citations.

Using the scroll bar on the right side of the screen enables you to read the entire text of the document shown. However, a more efficient method of determining whether the document is relevant to your issue is to use the "Term" arrows within the document itself.

Note the terms in your issue statement within the document. They will be shown in bold with arrows before and after the term. If you wish to see the next page containing your search terms, click the right arrow in the "Term" box in the upper-right portion of the page, and it will take you to the next page where the requirements of your query were met if you have used a Terms & Connectors search. If you have used a Natural Language search, clicking the arrow will move you to the part of the document that most closely matches your description.

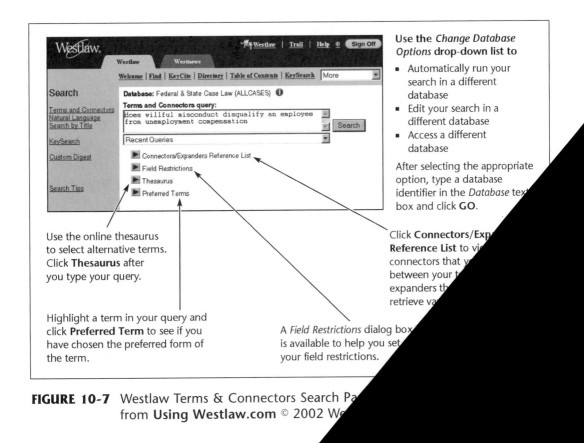

FIGURE 10-7 Westlaw Terms & Connectors Search Pa
from **Using Westlaw.com** © 2002 We

If you wish to find the portion of the document that most closely matches your Natural Language description, click the "Best" arrow in the upper-right portion of the screen. You will be able to move to the five closest matches to your issue description.

A reference guide for browsing documents is shown in Figure 10-8 on pages 133–134.

HYPERTEXT LINKS

You may already be familiar with using hypertext links to move from one document to another. These links are provided within your retrieved documents to enable you to immediately go to case law, law review articles, headnotes, state statutes, court rules, and other information. If you see an underlined name in a different color in your document, click on it to go to the material referenced in the hyperlink.

For instance, if you are reading the case headnotes, you will notice that each numbered headnote is a hypertext link. Clicking on the link will take you to the portion of the court decision where that particular headnote is discussed.

~ING LOCATE FUNCTION

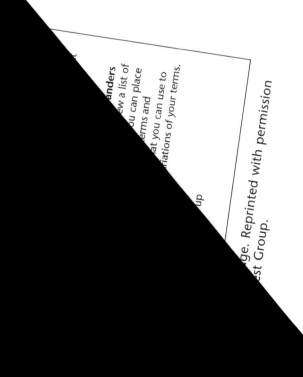

the left frame of your screen. Select "Locate" formulate a Locate request as find the portions of the docu- query. Use the Term arrows to Locate terms. You may exit the te" from the drop-down list in

ie United States may be found on e-blank" templates, you can access ngs, liens, judgments, lawsuits, and enables you to find people by their the Asset Locator, you can find real l property transfers, foreclosures, re- cords, and stock locator records.

Browsing Within a Document	
If you want to move	**Then**
Screen by screen	Click below the scroll box in the scroll bar.
Line by line	Click the down scroll arrow.
By scrolling	Position your cursor on the down scroll arrow and hold down the mouse button.
To an approximate page	Drag the scroll box along the scroll bar to the page's approximate position.
To the next occurrence of your search terms	Click a **Term** arrow to move between pages containing your search terms.
To terms not necessarily included in your search	Select **Locate** from the drop-down list in the left frame and click **GO**. In the *Locate Query* text box, type the terms you want to locate (formulated as a Terms and Connectors query) and click **Locate**.
To the part of the document that most closely matches your Natural Language description	Use the **Best** arrows.
From a case headnote to the corresponding text in the opinion	Click the headnote number.

Moving Between Documents	
If you want to view	**Then**
The next document in your search result	From the citations list in the left frame of the Search Result page, click the document's retrieval number.
A specific document in your search result	From the citations list in the left frame of the Search Result page, click the retrieval number of the case you want to retrieve.
The previous or next group of documents in your search result	Click the **Prev** and **Next** buttons in the left frame of the Search Result page.

FIGURE 10-8 Reference Guide to Browsing Documents in Westlaw. Reprinted with permission from *Legal Research Using Westlaw* © 2001 West Group.

Moving Between Documents	
If you want to view	**Then**
The next document in sequence even though it was not retrieved by your search or Find request (e.g., the next sequential statute)	Click the **Docs in Seq** button at the bottom of the right frame. To cancel, click the **Cancel Docs in Seq** button.
A cited document	Click the hypertext link.
The table of contents (for a statute, regulation, or rule)	Click the **TOC** tab.
Update information (for a statute, regulation, or rule)	Click the **KC History** tab.

FIGURE 10-8 *(continued)*

All of this information is accessible via the Westlaw home page. The following list provides some of the records available, as well as their database identification:

Business and Corporate Filings	*Database*
Corporate and limited partnership records	CORP-ALL
Corporate and limited partnership records by state* (does not include NJ and DE)	XX-CORP
Business Finder records—U.S.	BUSFIND-US
Business Finder records by state*	XX-BUSFIND

UCC Filings, Liens, and Judgments	
Combined UCC filings, liens, civil judgment filings	ULJ-ALL
By State*	XX-ULJ
Lien records by state*	XX-LJ

People Finder	
People Finder—Track by Name	PEOPLE-NAME
People Tracker by Name—Individual States*	XX-PEOPLE

---

* XX is the state's postal abbreviation

Bankruptcy Records	*Database*
Combined records	BKR-ALL
Combined records by state*	XX-BKR

Lawsuit Records	
Combined records	LS-ALL
Combined records by state*	XX-LS

Asset Locator	
Real property assessor's records	RPA-ALL
Real property assessor's records by state*	XX-RPA
Real property asset transfers	RPT-ALL
Real property asset transfers by state*	XX-RPT
Real property foreclosures	RPF-ALL
Real property foreclosures by state*	XX-RPF

A full listing of all public records accessible from Westlaw may be found in the *Westlaw Database Directory.*

Corporate law offices will find the Business and Corporate Filings extremely valuable in those cases where it is necessary to obtain financial information about a corporate adverse party in a lawsuit. The People Finder might prove valuable in searching for those elusive individuals who are avoiding service or the payment of a judgment against them. The Asset Locator might prove to be useful in finding assets to attach for those opposing parties who owe the client money damages from an adverse judgment.

SPECIALIZED CASE LAW DATABASES

In addition to the ability to find the actual case, the Westlaw system gives you editorial enhancements that provide accurate and complete information on that particular case. This system is called Full-Text Plus format; it includes the following information in addition to the actual court opinion:

1. *Synopsis field (sy)*—includes a summary of the case. The summary consists of a review of the facts of the case as well as the lower court judge's name and decision, the court's holding in the case itself, the name of the judge who wrote the court's opinion, any other judges who wrote or joined in dissenting or concurring opinions, and a syllabus of the case that has been prepared by the court, if available.

2. *Digest field (di)*—includes the headnotes and topics covered in the case.

3. *Topic field (to)*—includes the West key numbers that enable you to find cases with headnotes classified under a West digest topic. These topics have been separated into legal issues for identification purposes by West. Each issue is assigned a topic and key number classification.

4. *Headnote field (he)*—includes headnotes for each point of law being decided in a case. Summaries are provided for each point of law in the case itself.

Figure 10-9 shows a typical case as it appears in the case law database. The various parts of the case are labeled as discussed above.

Methods of searching each of these parts of the database are discussed next. You may restrict your search to only one field or to a combination of fields.

Digest Field Search

Use a digest field search when your terms have common words or multiple meanings. The digest field search enables you to limit your search to the law in the digest. You are then able to find cases even if your request uses different terms from those used by the court in its decision.

In order to search by the digest field alone, perform the following steps:

1. Go to the Terms & Connectors search page.
2. Click "Field Restrictions."
3. Select "Digest DI" from the drop-down list.
4. Type your search terms.
5. Click "Go."

If you wish to restrict your search terms to the same paragraph, use the connector for paragraph between your search terms **(/p)**.

Alternatively, just as in the synopsis field search, you may type

di

after your search terms in the query box to access the digest field.

In some cases, you may wish to search the synopsis and digest fields simultaneously. This technique is useful for finding only those cases where your terms are important. You may accomplish this task by typing

sy, di

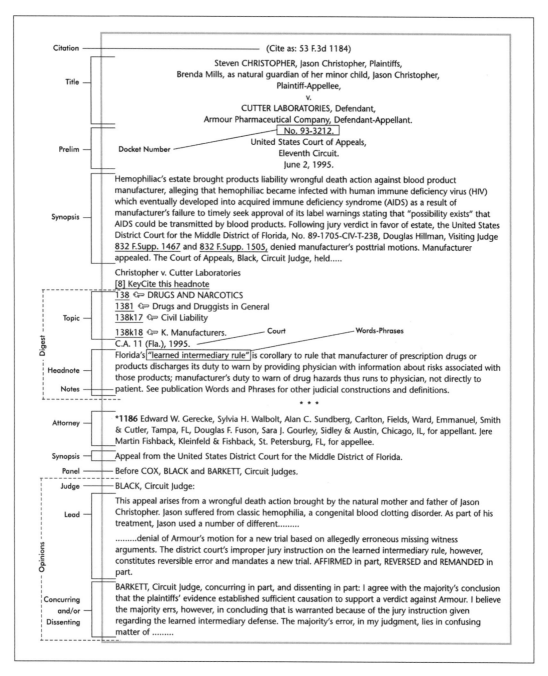

FIGURE 10-9 Case Law Fields on Westlaw. Reprinted with permission from *Discovering Westlaw* © 2000 West Group.

before your search terms. Figure 10-10 on pages 139–141 contains a typical search page for a digest field search.

Topic Searches

West assigns topics and key numbers to all cases reported in its national reporter system. By the use of these topics and key numbers, you may use West's publications and Westlaw together to find material. Restrict your search to West Digest topics or key numbers by following these directions:

1. Go to the Terms & Connectors search page.
2. Click "Field Restrictions."
3. Find the dialog box and select "Topic TO" from the drop-down list.
4. Type your search terms in parentheses.
5. Click "Go."

Alternatively, you may also type

to

after your initial search terms in the Terms & Connectors box. If you wish to use a key number instead of a digest topic, use the number after the "**to**." For example, you might use either

to(134)

or

to(divorce)

to find cases with headnotes for Topic 134, Divorce. If you wish to find cases on two different topics, type both key numbers in the parentheses. This search method is valuable for finding cases that discuss a certain specialty area of the law.

Searches by Hypertext Links

Hypertext links are provided within the case headnotes to enable you to retrieve all headnotes in the appropriate jurisdiction that include that particular topic and key number. If you click the topic and key number in which you are interested, you will be taken to the Key Search Page, a copy of which is shown in Figure 10-11 on pages 141–142.

Note that the jurisdiction displayed will always be your home jurisdiction. In the preceding example, the home jurisdiction is the state of

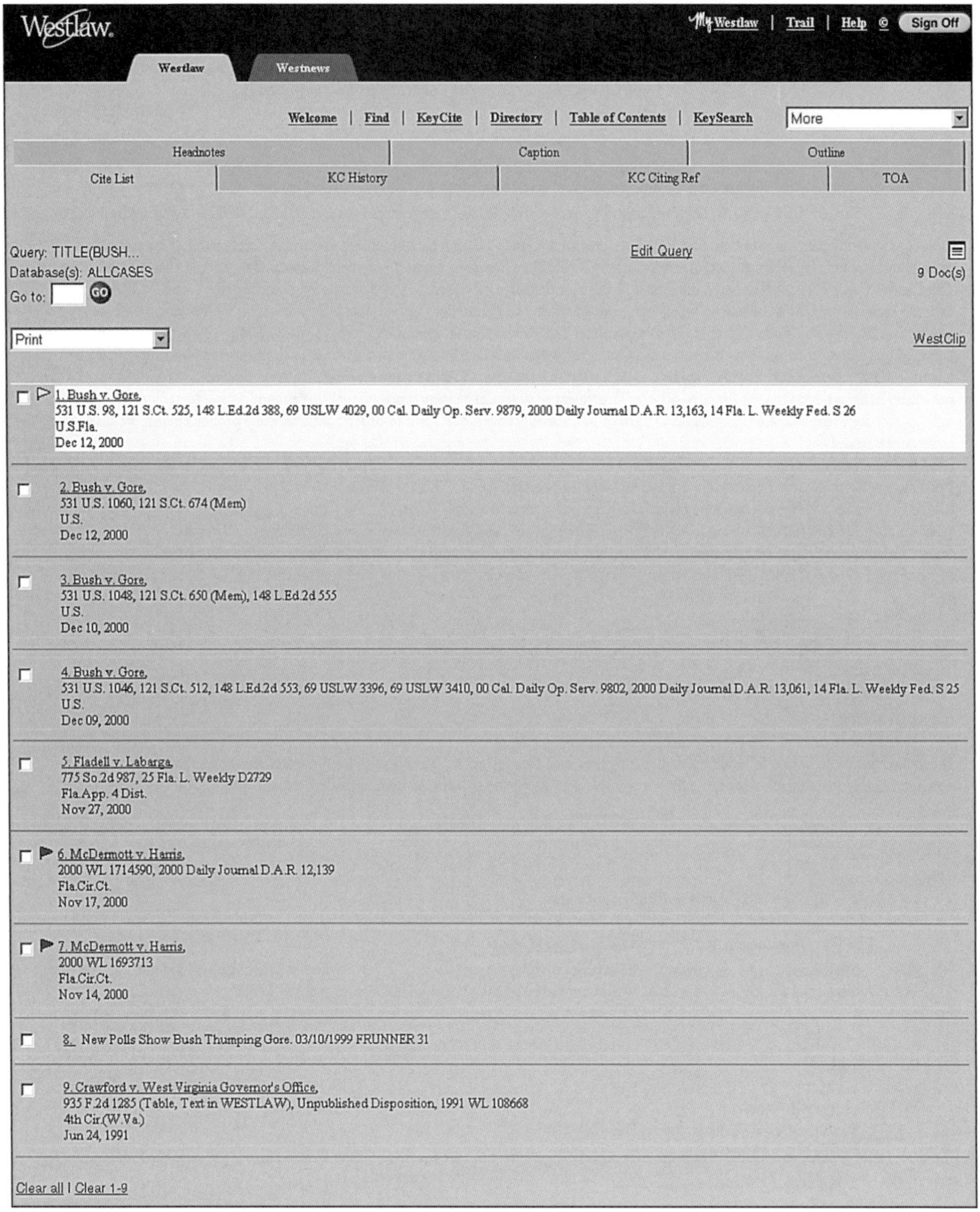

FIGURE 10-10 Digest Field Search Page. Reprinted with permission from
Westlaw.com © 2002 West Group.

Westlaw.   *My* Westlaw | Trail | Help © Sign Off

Westlaw   Westnews

Welcome | Find | KeyCite | Directory | Table of Contents | KeySearch   More

Case

Bush v. Gore
121 S.Ct. 525
U.S.Fla.,2000.
Dec. 12, 2000. (Approx. 27 pages)

WEST
GROUP

148 L.Ed.2d 388, 69 USLW 4029, 00 Cal. Daily Op. Serv. 9879, 2000 Daily Journal D.A.R. 13,163, 14 Fla. L. Weekly Fed. S 26

Democratic candidates for President and Vice President of the United States filed complaint contesting certification of state results in presidential election. The Circuit Court, Leon County, N. Sanders Sauls, J., entered judgment denying all relief, and candidates appealed. The District Court of Appeal certified the matter to the Florida Supreme Court. On review, the Florida Supreme Court, 772 So.2d 1243, ordered manual recounts of ballots on which machines had failed to detect vote for President. Republican candidates filed emergency application for stay of Florida Supreme Court's mandate. The United States Supreme Court, 531 U.S. 1046, 121 S.Ct. 512, 148 L.Ed.2d 553, granted application, treating it as petition for writ of certiorari, and granted certiorari. The Supreme Court held that: (1) manual recounts ordered by Florida Supreme Court, without specific standards to implement its order to discern "intent of the voter," did not satisfy minimum requirement for non-arbitrary treatment of voters necessary, under Equal Protection Clause, to secure fundamental right to vote for President, and (2) remand of case to Florida Supreme Court for it to order constitutionally proper contest would not be appropriate remedy.

Reversed and remanded.

Chief Justice Rehnquist filed concurring opinion in which Justices Scalia and Thomas joined.

Justice Stevens filed dissenting opinion in which Justices Ginsburg and Breyer joined.

Justice Souter filed dissenting opinion in which Justice Breyer joined and Justices Stevens and Ginsburg joined in part.

Justice Ginsburg filed dissenting opinion in which Justice Stevens joined and Justices Souter and Breyer joined in part.

Justice Breyer filed dissenting opinion in which Justices Stevens and Ginsburg joined in part, and in which Justice Souter also joined in part.

West Headnotes

[1] KeyCite Notes

⟸393 United States
　　⟸393I Government in General
　　　　⟸393k25 k. Presidential Electors. Most Cited Cases

The individual citizen has no federal constitutional right to vote for electors for President of the United States unless and until state legislature chooses statewide election as means to implement its power to appoint members of Electoral College. U.S.C.A. Const. Art. 2, § 1, cl. 2.

[2] KeyCite Notes

⟸144 Elections
　　⟸144I Right of Suffrage and Regulation Thereof in General
　　　　⟸144k8 Statutory Provisions Conferring or Defining Right
　　　　　　⟸144k10 k. Construction and Operation. Most Cited Cases

When state legislature vests right to vote for President in its people, the right to vote as legislature has prescribed is fundamental, and one source of its fundamental nature lies in the equal weight accorded to each vote and equal dignity owed to each voter. U.S.C.A. Const. Art. 2, § 1; Art. 2, cl. 2.

[3] KeyCite Notes

⟸393 United States
　　⟸393I Government in General
　　　　⟸393k25 k. Presidential Electors. Most Cited Cases

The State, after granting individual citizens the right to vote for electors for the President of the United States, can take back the power to appoint electors. U.S.C.A. Const. Art. 2, § 1, cl. 2.

FIGURE 10-10 *(continued)*

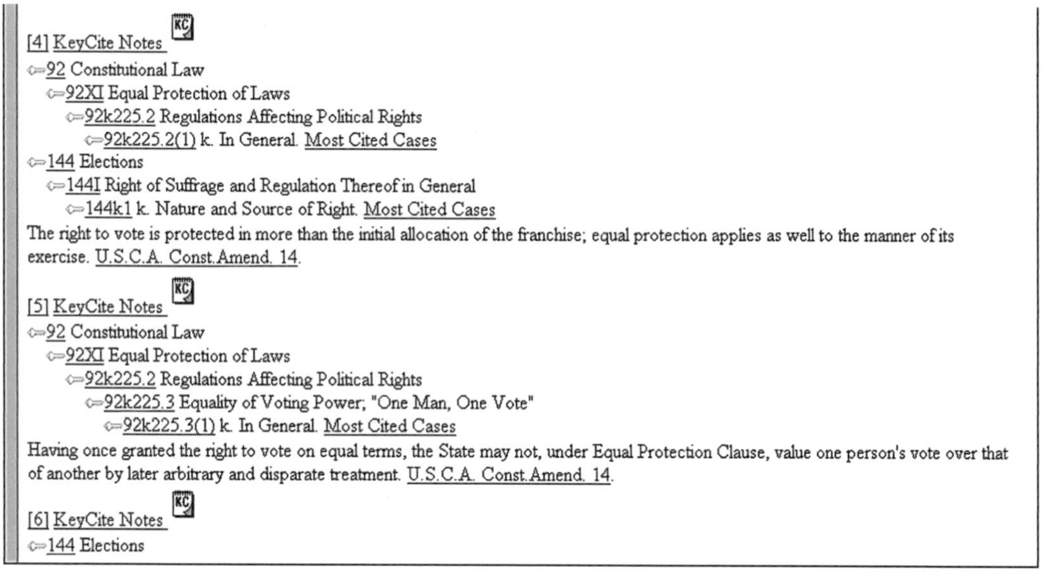

[4] KeyCite Notes ![KC]

☞92 Constitutional Law
   ☞92XI Equal Protection of Laws
      ☞92k225.2 Regulations Affecting Political Rights
         ☞92k225.2(1) k. In General. Most Cited Cases
☞144 Elections
   ☞144I Right of Suffrage and Regulation Thereof in General
      ☞144k1 k. Nature and Source of Right. Most Cited Cases
The right to vote is protected in more than the initial allocation of the franchise; equal protection applies as well to the manner of its exercise. U.S.C.A. Const.Amend. 14.

[5] KeyCite Notes ![KC]

☞92 Constitutional Law
   ☞92XI Equal Protection of Laws
      ☞92k225.2 Regulations Affecting Political Rights
         ☞92k225.3 Equality of Voting Power; "One Man, One Vote"
            ☞92k225.3(1) k. In General. Most Cited Cases
Having once granted the right to vote on equal terms, the State may not, under Equal Protection Clause, value one person's vote over that of another by later arbitrary and disparate treatment. U.S.C.A. Const.Amend. 14.

[6] KeyCite Notes ![KC]

☞144 Elections

FIGURE 10-10   *(continued)*

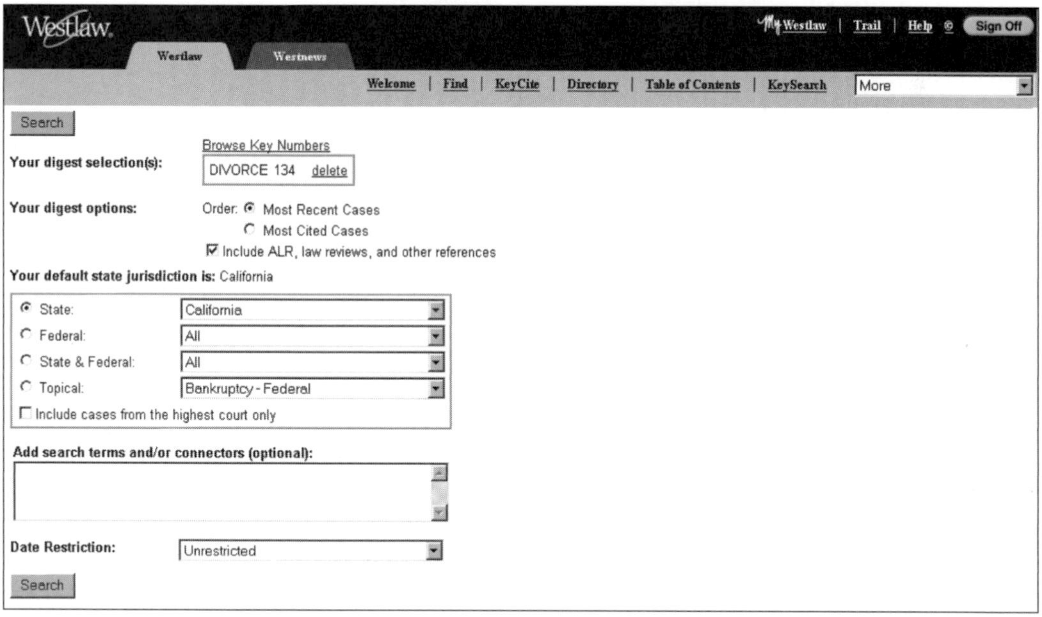

FIGURE 10-11   Westlaw Key Search Page. Reprinted with permission from **Westlaw.com** © 2002 West Group.

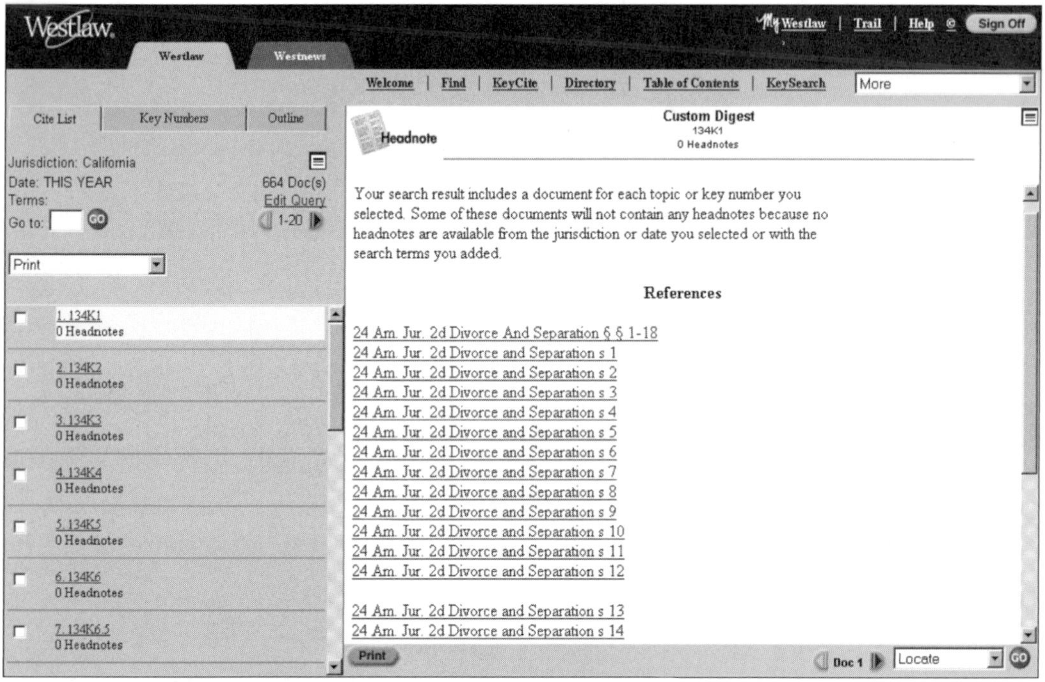

FIGURE 10-11 *(continued)*

Minnesota. If you wish to find material from other jurisdictions, you must so indicate by choosing an entry from the drop-down list.

You may also add additional terms to your search at this point. Type these terms in the box for "Additional Terms." The search will indicate those cases in the particular jurisdiction indicated.

Updating Key Numbers

From time to time old key numbers are changed, deleted, or modified. New key numbers are added to accommodate the changes in the law. Your search will automatically take these changes into account so that if you enter an obsolete key number, Westlaw will update it to the revised number. In those cases, your search will indicate a new key number directly above the old one, with the word "Formerly" indicated next to the old key number. "Formerly" appears in the middle of the page under "Conspiracies" indicating the former number for Conspiracies as well as the new one. Figure 10-12 shows a Westlaw headnote with a "Formerly" line.

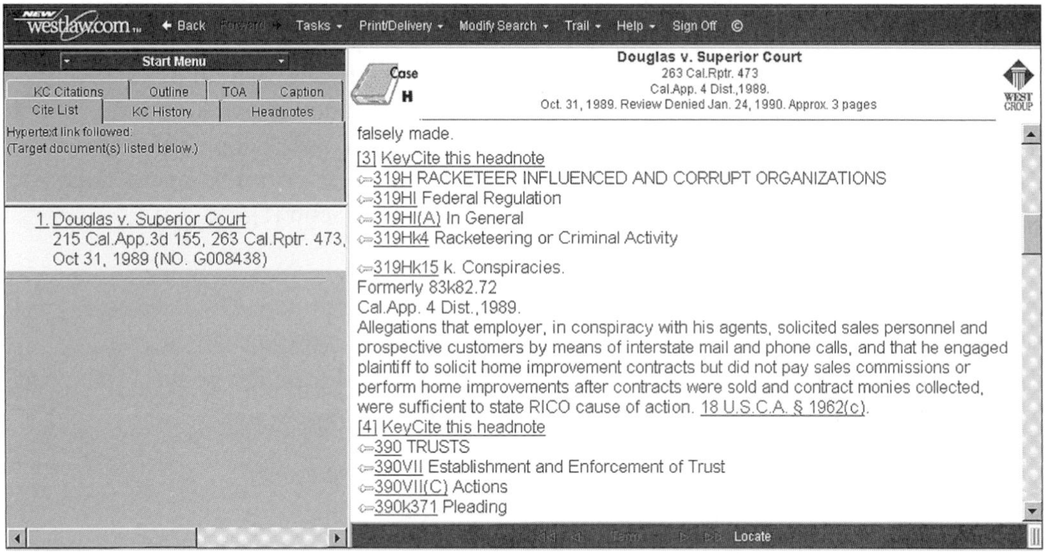

FIGURE 10-12 Westlaw Headnote with "Formerly" Line. Reprinted with permission from *Discovering Westlaw* © 2000 West Group.

Table of Authorities Service

The Table of Authorities service enables you to find all other cases that have been cited by your case. It is a useful tool for determining if there are hidden weaknesses in the case you are using, because it lists all cases on which the case you are using relied. It also shows any significant negative history of those cases. You can access the Table of Authorities service by the following steps:

1. Note the drop-down list at the top of the page.
2. Select "Table of Authorities" and click "Go."
3. The Table of Authorities page will be displayed.
4. Type the case citation in the "Enter a citation" box and click "Go."

Cases will be listed by their citations and depth of history. Cases with a negative history are marked with red or yellow flags; those with a positive history are marked with green flags.

Each number in the front of the citation represents a hyperlink to that case. Click the number of the case to view it.

SEARCHING STATUTES DATABASES

Westlaw enables you to search for both state and federal statutes and, in addition, to find historical notes and annotations to assist you in explanations and applications of the statute. You may use "Scope" for basic information for research into statutes as well as descriptions of the database. This field is accessible by clicking the Scope icon (I).

Find Feature

If you know the exact number of the statute for which you are searching, use the following method to access the statute:

1. Find the drop-down list at the top of the page.
2. Click on "Find a Document" from the list.
3. Click on "Go".
4. Type in the appropriate code for the statute being sought.

Specific instructions for retrieving federal and state statutes follow:

1. Retrieving federal statutes
   a. Go to the "Enter a citation" text box.
   b. Enter the citation.
   c. Click "Go."
   For example, to retrieve 22 U.S.C.A. Sec. 11199, type

   22 usca s 11199

   and click "Go."

2. Retrieving state statutes
   a. Go to the "Enter a citation" text box.
   b. Type in the state's postal abbreviation, statute abbreviation, and section.
   c. Click "Go."
   For example, to retrieve a state statute for Florida with the number 222.11, type

   fl st s 222.11

   and click "Go."

3. Retrieving a state code (statute)

   a. Go to the "Enter a citation" text box.

   b. Type the state's postal abbreviation, code name or abbreviation, and code section number.

   c. Click "Go."

   For example, to retrieve Section 211 of the Penal Code of California, type

   ca p s 211

4. Retrieving a state constitution

   a. Go to the "Enter a citation" text box.

   b. Type in the state abbreviation, constitution abbreviation, article and section numbers.

   c. Click "Go."

   For example, to find Article 3, Section 9 of the Florida State Constitution, type:

   fl const art 3 s 9

A few states include both title and section numbers in their statutes. To retrieve one of their statutes, step 2 above must include both the title and section number of the statute. For example, to find Title 22, Section 333, of Oklahoma State Statutes, type

ok st ti 22 s 333

Searching without the Citation

When you do not know the citation for a statute, you can do a descriptive word search by either the Terms & Connectors or Natural Language method.

Searching in an annotated statutes database will enable you to find how the statute has been construed and to obtain other information, including cases related to that particular statute. This method is particularly useful when you are searching for a term that is not usually found in statutory language.

Searching with Table of Contents Service

When you are interested in viewing not only a particular statute but also those statutes surrounding it, the Table of Contents service will provide those other statutes for you. This service is available for the following statutes:

1. United States Code Annotated (USCA)
2. Uniform Laws Annotated (ULA)
3. State statutes and rules (XX-ST)*
4. State administrative codes (XX-ADQ)*

Follow the following directions for finding statutes using this service:

1. Go to the drop-down list and select "Table of Contents Service."
2. Click "Go."
3. Type the appropriate abbreviation for the material you wish to view.
4. Click "Go."

For example, if you wish to view the United States Code Annotated, you would type

usca

in step 3 above. If you wish to see all items available in the Table of Contents service, click "Abbreviations List" on the left side of the page.

You can also gain access to the Table of Contents service from a statute you are reading on your screen. If you click a heading in the statute's caption field, it will take you to the service. See Figures 10-13, 10-14 on page 148, and 10-15 on page 149 for the pages just described.

Items available on the Table of Contents service include the following:

1. Code of Federal Regulations
2. United States Code Annotated
3. Uniform Laws Annotated
4. State Statutes
5. Court rules
6. Administrative materials

In some cases, you may retrieve a statute that has been either amended or repealed. If so, you will see an "Update" message in the statute itself. To see the legislation that either amends or repeals your statute, click the "Update" hyperlink, and you will be taken to the new legislation.

New statutes can be retrieved via a legislative service database. These databases include laws that were passed during the present session of the

---

* XX indicates the abbreviation for the particular state.

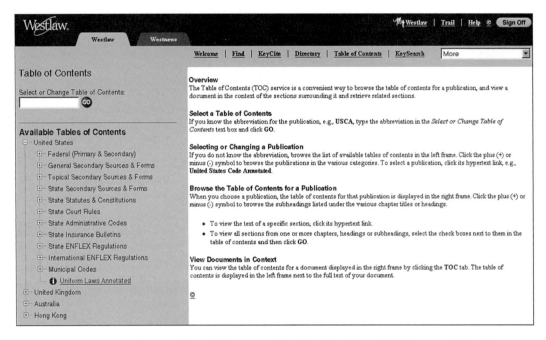

FIGURE 10-13 Westlaw Table of Contents Service. Reprinted with permission from
Westlaw.com © 2002 West Group.

legislature. They cannot be accessed via the Update link. Therefore, other
methods must be used to update some of your research on statutes.

In those cases where a new statute has been enacted, it will be necessary
to access a legislative service database and run a search using the appropriate issue being sought. To determine other uses of the legislative service
database, or to find other databases dealing with statutes, use the Scope
feature described earlier.

SPECIALIZED SEARCHES—SECONDARY SOURCES

In some cases, more general information is required in your research. Secondary sources (those representing persuasive authority or commentary)
may be accessed for explanations of legal principles in various fields.
These sources are very useful for those situations in which the researcher
is unfamiliar with that area of the law and wishes to learn about that specialty and to find references to primary sources dealing with that practice
area. Westlaw provides access to several hundred law reviews, state bar

FIGURE 10-14 Statute Headings. Reprinted with permission from **Westlaw.com**
© 2002 West Group.

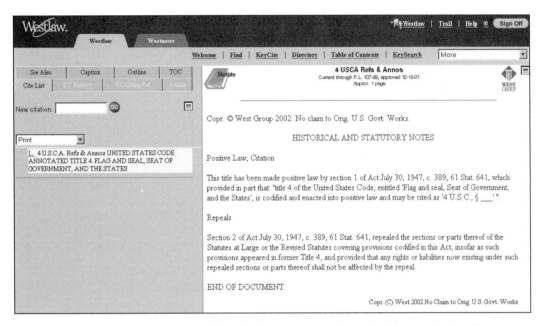

FIGURE 10-15 Title 4, USCA, Table Of Contents. Reprinted with permission from **Westlaw.com** © 2002 West Group.

journals, course materials for continuing legal education, and newspapers for this type of research.

Several different types of databases are available to aid in your search of secondary sources. General databases provide a broad search capability in various secondary sources, such as textbooks, periodicals, law reviews, journals, newspapers, and other general information sources. Specialty databases provide information by law-specialty subject area, such as bankruptcy, estate planning, and family law. In addition, each journal and law review has its own database dating back to 1980. Figure 10-16 on page 150 shows a page of the Westlaw database directory for law reviews and bar journals.

Following are the identifiers for some of the general databases:

Database	Identifier
Law reviews, textbooks, and bar journals	TP-ALL
State journals and law reviews	XX-JLR*
American Bar Association journals	AMBAR-TP
American Law Institute of the ABA— continuing legal education	ALI-ABA

* XX = state's abbreviation; i.e., CA-JLR would search for California's state bar journals.

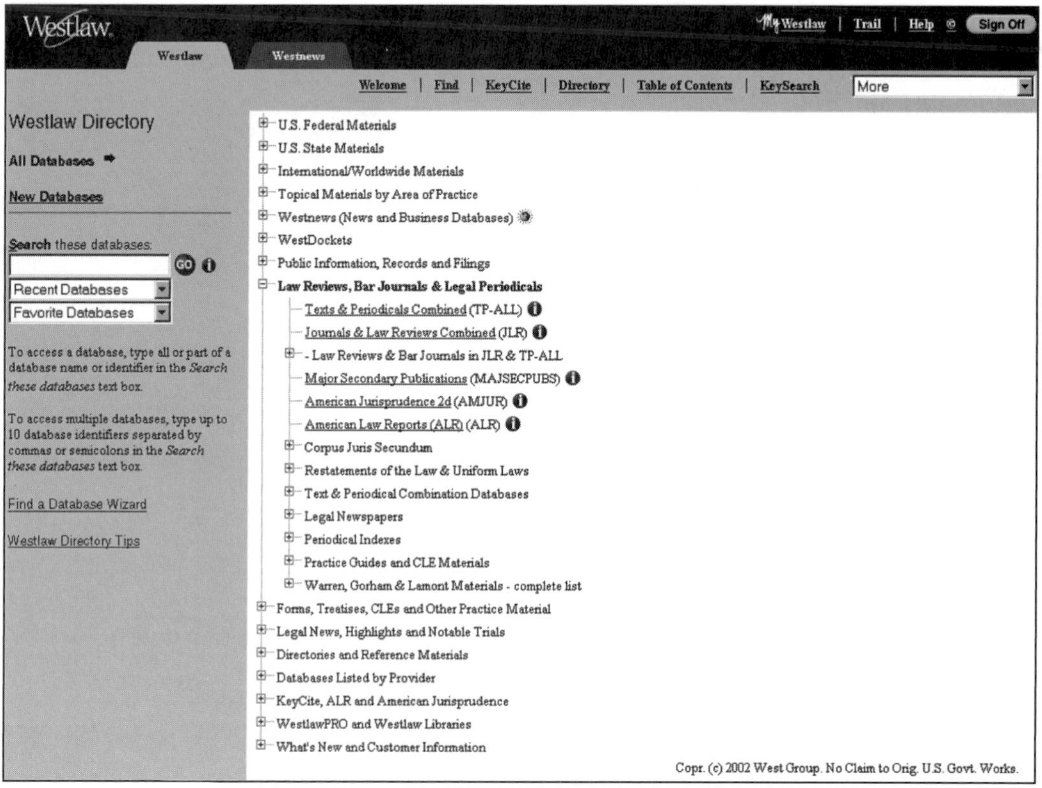

FIGURE 10-16 Westlaw Law Reviews and Bar Journals Directory. Reprinted with permission from **Westlaw.com** © 2002 West Group.

Database	Identifier
Textbooks and treatises on the law	TEXTS
United States newspapers	PAPERS
	PAPERS2
National Law Journal	NLJ

A list of those databases that are available in various practice areas is included in Figure 10-17 on pages 151–152. A list of databases for texts and treatises on the law, including all of the Restatement of the law, is given in Figure 10-18 on pages 152–153. Note that these lists do not include all available databases. The online Westlaw Directory or the printed *Westlaw Database Directory* will give a complete list of all available secondary-sources databases.

Database Name	Identifier
Administrative Law	AD-TP
Antitrust & Trade Regulation	ATR-TP
Bankruptcy	BKR-TP
Business Organizations	BUS-TP
Civil Rights	CIV-TP
Commercial Law & Contracts	CML-TP
Communications	COM-TP
Criminal Justice	CJ-TP
Education	ED-TP
Energy	EN-TP
Environmental Law	ENV-TP
Estate Planning & Probate	EPP-TP
Family Law	FL-TP
Finance & Banking	FIN-TP
First Amendment	CFA-TP
Government Benefits	GB-TP
Government Contracts	GC-TP
Health Law	HTH-TP
Immigration Law	IM-TP
Insurance	IN-TP
Intellectual Property	IP-TP
International Law	INT-TP
Jurisprudence & Constitutional Theory	JCT-TP
Labor & Employment	LB-TP
Legal Ethics & Professional Responsibility	ETH-TP

FIGURE 10-17 Westlaw Specialty Topics Databases. Reprinted with permission from *Discovering Westlaw* © 2000 West Group.

Database Name	Identifier
Litigation	LTG-TP
Maritime Law	MRT-TP
Military Law	MIL-TP
Native Americans Law	NAM-TP
Pension & Retirement Benefits	PEN-TP
Products Liability	PL-TP
Professional Malpractice	MAL-TP
Real Property	RP-TP
Securities and Blue Sky Law	SEC-TP
Taxation	TX-TP
Tort Law	TRT-TP
Transportation	TRAN-TP
Workers' Compensation	WC-TP

FIGURE 10-17   *(continued)*

Database Name	Identifier
American Jurisprudence 2d (Am Jur 2d)	AMJUR
American Law Reports	ALR
Clean Air Act: Law and Practice	JW-CLEANAIR
Couch on Insurance	COUCH
Environmental Law	ENVLAW
Federal Jury Practice and Instructions	FED-JI
Federal Practice and Procedure (Wright & Miller)	FPP
Federal Sentencing Law and Practice	FSLP
Federal Tax Practice (Casey)	CASEY
Handbook of Federal Evidence	FEDEVID

FIGURE 10-18   Westlaw Restatement, Text, and Treatise Databases.
Reprinted with permission from *Discovering Westlaw*
© 2000 West Group.

Database Name	Identifier
Handbook on Insurance Coverage Disputes	ICD
Hazardous Waste Law and Practice	JW-HAZWASTE
Insurance Law and Practice (Appleman's)	APPLEMAN
Law of Federal Income Taxation (Mertens)	MERTENS
Manual for Complex Litigation, Third Edition	MCL
Modern Intellectual Property, Second Edition	MODIP
Principles of Corporate Governance: Analysis and Recommendations	ALI-CORPGOV
Punitive Damages: A State-by-State Guide to Law and Practice	PUNITIVE
Restatements of the Law	REST
Agency	REST-AGEN
Conflict of Laws	REST-CONFL
Contracts	REST-CONTR
The Foreign Relations Law of the United States	REST-FOREL
Judgments	REST-JUDG
The Law Governing Lawyers	REST-LGOVL
Property	REST-PROP
Restitution	REST-RESTI
Security and Suretyship and Guaranty	REST-SEC
Torts	REST-TORT
Trusts	REST-TRUST
Unfair Competition	REST-UNCOM
Search and Seizure: A Treatise on the Fourth Amendment	SEARCHSZR
Treatise on Constitutional Law: Substance and Procedure	CONLAW
Uniform Commercial Code Series (Hawkland)	HAWKLAND
Witkin's California Treatises	WITKIN

FIGURE 10-18 *(continued)*

Index to Legal Periodicals/Legal Resource Index Databases

The Index to Legal Periodicals (ILP) and the Legal Resource Index (LRI) contain lists of articles on given subjects from all over the world. You can access the database and use a Natural Language search method to search for all articles on a particular subject. For instance, if you wish to find articles on surrogate parenting in the LRI database you would perform the following steps:

1. Access the LRI database.
2. Note that you wish to use the Natural Language search method.
3. Enter the following explanation in the terms field:

   surrogate parenting

You will be able to retrieve all articles on surrogate parenting that have appeared in journals in the United States, Great Britain, Australia, Canada, New Zealand, and Ireland. See Figure 10-19 for a sample search result using the LRI.

Law Review Articles

Just as statutes and cases can be retrieved using "Find," law review articles can also be found in this manner, provided you know the citation for the law review article.

To find a law review article using this feature, perform the following steps:

1. From the top of the page, select "Find a document" from the drop-down list.
2. Click "Go."
3. Note the "Enter a citation" box.
4. Type the citation for the law review article you are seeking.

If that particular law review is not available, another page indicating whether the article summary can be accessed in the LRI or the ILP database will be shown.

In order to determine whether the particular publication in which you are interested is accessible, you can also use the "Find" feature:

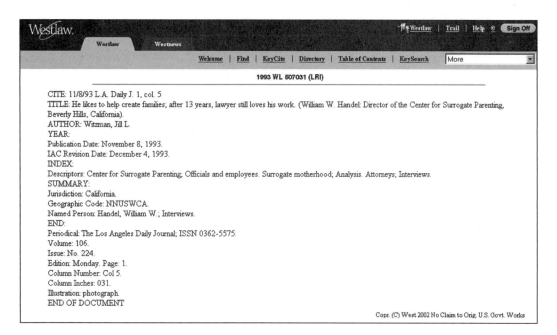

FIGURE 10-19 Westlaw Legal Resource Index Search Result. Reprinted with permission from **Westlaw.com** © 2002 West Group.

1. Select "Find."
2. Click "Publications List" on the left side of the screen.
3. A list of all publications available on Westlaw will be shown.

To find a list of only law reviews accessible, click the "Contains" button on the top of the page after performing the preceding three steps. When the text box appears, type

law reviews

and click "Scan." A sample page using this feature is shown in Figure 10-20 on page 156.

Several other search methods are available for publications. You can search for articles by the author's name, the title of the article, or by subject. These methods were discussed earlier for statutes and cases. They are the same method for articles or publications.

To utilize these procedures for searching, you must first access the appropriate publication or law review database. Once the database has been found, use these steps to find the article in which you are interested.

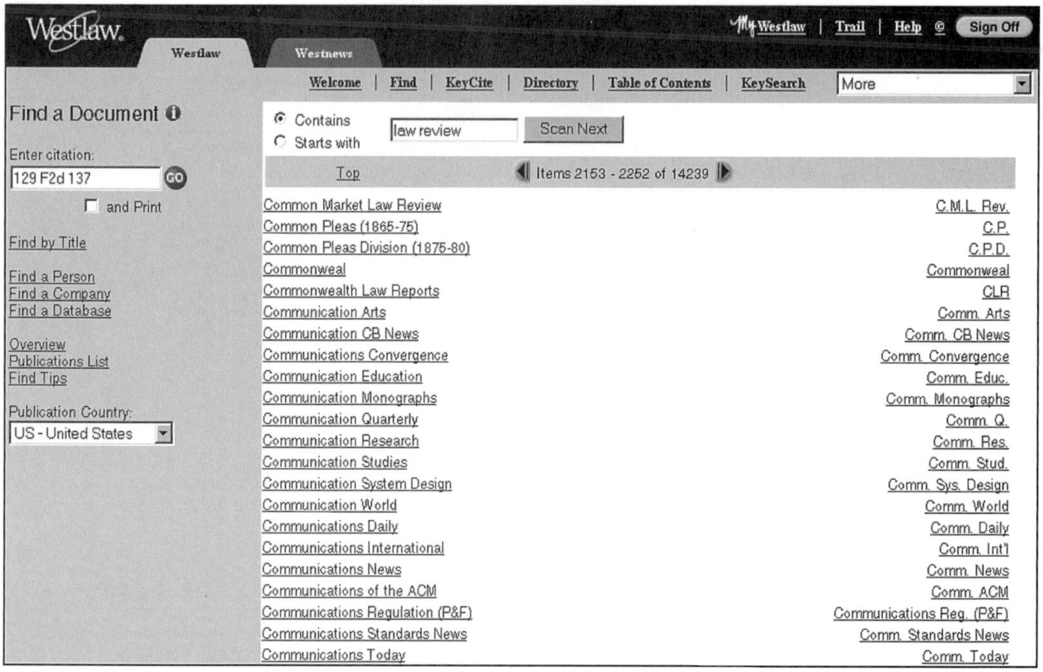

FIGURE 10-20   Law Reviews Search Using Scan. Reprinted with permission from **Westlaw.com** © 2002 West Group.

1. Author's Name
   a. Access the appropriate database.
   b. Select the appropriate search method.
   c. Restrict your search to the author field **(au)**.
   d. Enter your query for the author.
2. Title of Article
   a. Access the appropriate database.
   b. Select the appropriate search method.
   c. Restrict your search to the title field **(ti)**.
   d. Enter your query for the name of the article.
3. Subject of Article
   a. Access the appropriate database.
   b. Select the appropriate search method.
   c. Type in a description of the subject in which you are interested.

You may need to review the search procedures for Natural Language and Terms & Connectors.

Often when you are reading a case or law review article, you will find a hypertext link to another article. You can instantly access that article by clicking on the hypertext link.

HIGHLIGHTS DATABASES

On occasion you will wish to view the recent legal developments in a given area of law, in a certain state, or from the United States Supreme Court. The following databases enable you to conduct this type of search:

1. *Westlaw Bulletin (WLB)*—This database provides a brief description of recent cases on the state and federal levels.

2. *Topical Highlights*—Descriptions are provided for recent cases in given legal specialty areas, such as probate, family law, or bankruptcy.

3. *State Bulletins*—Significant cases decided by specific states are described.

4. *Westlaw Bulletin for the United States Supreme Court (WLB-SCT)*—Recent Supreme Court issues and developments are provided, as well as cases, orders, and court rules.

For additional lists of Topical Highlights databases, see the online Westlaw directory.

NEWS AND GENERAL INFORMATION DATABASES

Sometimes you must search more general information to provide you with background information and foundational data. Many general sources are available on Westlaw to assist you, including newspapers, newswires, newsletters, journals, and magazines. Over 100 newspapers may be accessed via Westlaw. Figure 10-21 on pages 158–160 provides a chart of most of these databases. A complete directory of all such databases available on Westlaw can be found on the online Westlaw Directory or the *Westlaw Data Directory*. To obtain a detailed description of the database, see "Scope."

Legal Newspapers		
Database Name	**Identifier**	**Start of Coverage**
Chicago Daily Law Bulletin	CHIDLB	May 1991
The Chicago Lawyer	CHIL	April 1991
Corporate Legal Times	CORPLT	Fall 1991
Daily Record (Baltimore, MD)	DAILYREC	Aug. 1991
Daily Reporter (Milwaukee)	DAIL-REPT	Aug. 1988
Journal Record (Oklahoma City)	JROKC	April 1985
Legal Newspapers (Multibase)	LEGALNP	Varies by publication
Massachusetts Lawyers Weekly	MLW	May 1991
Merrill's Illinois Legal Times	ILLT	Jan. 1990
The Metropolitan Corporate Counsel	METCC	Feb. 1997
The National Law Journal	NLJ	Oct. 1989
New York Law Journal	NYLJ	April 1990

Combined Newspaper Databases*	
Database Name	**Identifier**
Combined U.S. Newspaper Database	PAPERS, PAPERS2
United States Papers	USNP
Dow Jones Major Newspapers	NPMJ
Major U.S. Newspaper Database*	PAPERSMJ
Newspapers	NP
Newspapers Plus	NPPLUS
Same-Day Newspapers Business Coverage	BSX-NP
State Papers	XXNP (where XX is the state's two-letter postal abbreviation)
Newspapers Full Text—California*	PAPERSCA

FIGURE 10-21 Newspaper Databases. Reprinted with permission from *Discovering Westlaw* © 2000 West Group.

Combined Newspaper Databases*	
Database Name	**Identifier**
Newspapers Full Text—Colorado*	PAPERSCO
Newspapers Full Text—Florida*	PAPERSFL
Newspapers Full Text—Georgia*	PAPERSGA
Newspapers Full Text—Kentucky*	PAPERSKY
Newspapers Full Text—Minnesota*	PAPERSMN
Newspapers Full Text—Missouri*	PAPERSMO
Newspapers Full Text—New York*	PAPERSNY
Newspapers Full Text—Ohio*	PAPERSOH
Newspapers Full Text—Pennsylvania*	PAPERSPA
Newspapers Full Text—Tennessee*	PAPERSTN
Newspapers Full Text—Virginia*	PAPERSVA
Newspapers Full Text—Washington*	PAPERSWA
Newspapers Full Text—Washington D.C.*	PAPERSDC
Central U.S. Newspaper Database*	PAPERSCE
North Eastern U.S. Newspaper Database*	PAPERSNE
South Eastern U.S. Newspaper Database*	PAPERSSE
Western U.S. Newspaper Database*	PAPERSWE
Canada Papers	CANADANP
European and C.I.S. Newspapers	EURONP
Far East Newspapers	FARNP
Japan Papers	JAPANNP
New Zealand Newspapers*	PAPERSNZ
North American Newspapers	NORTHNP
United Kingdom Newspapers	UKNP

FIGURE 10-21   *(continued)*

Combined Newspaper Databases*	
Database Name	**Identifier**
Asia/Pacific News*	PAPERSAP
Canadian Newspapers*	PAPERSCAN
Latin American News*	PAPERSLAT
*A DIALOG on Westlaw newspaper database. You can limit your search to documents from the most recent 12 to 24 months by adding **-c** to the database identifier. For example, to search the most recent 12 to 24 months of *The Boston Globe*, type **bostglobe-c**.	

FIGURE 10-21   *(continued)*

Newspaper databases can provide information relevant to your issue by means of news stories related to lawsuits that have been settled. You can find information about a particular attorney, a particular lawsuit, a certain trial, or lawsuits involving a specific company.

NEWSWIRES

The Dow Jones newswire databases are particularly valuable to those attorneys dealing in international law, corporate law, government law, or finance. News about companies in the United States, Japan, Germany, Asia, and Canada can be found, including financial information and stock market data on those countries. Government law offices will find information about government agencies to be useful.

Detailed information about corporations is available, including the following:

1. Mergers and acquisitions
2. Tender offers
3. Proxies
4. Prospectuses
5. Leveraged buyouts
6. Current filings with the SEC

All Dow Jones databases are found in the Dow Jones Wires databa[...]
(WIRES). The individual databases are shown in the chart in Figure 10-2.

If you want to find news stories that were added to a particular database
within the last few hours, type "read" or "list" in the Terms & Connectors
query text box and only those articles will appear. When retrieving articles
about a given subject, you can restrict your search to a certain time period
or a particular area in the databases, such as the type of industry, ticker
symbol, or company name.

Database Name	Identifier
AFX News	AFX
Business Wire	BWIRE
Canada Newswire	CANWIRE
Canadian Corporate Newswire	CCWIRE
Capital Markets Report	CMREP
Deutsche Presse-Agentur (German Press Agency)	DCHPA
Dow Jones Asian Equities Report	DJAER
Dow Jones Australia and New Zealand Report	DJANZR
Dow Jones Commodities Service	DJCOMS
Dow Jones International News Service	DJINS
Dow Jones Money Management Alert	DJMMA
Dow Jones News Service	DJNS
Emerging Markets Report	EMREP
Japan Economic Newswire	JWIRE
PR Newswire	PRWIRE
Professional Investor Report	PIR
Select Federal Filings Newswires	FEDFILE

FIGURE 10-22 Dow Jones Newswire Databases. Reprinted with
permission from *Discovering Westlaw* © 2000 W[...]

One of the health law databases, such as MEDLINE, would be particularly useful to attorneys who practice in the area of medical malpractice. MEDLINE contains articles describing various medical procedures as well as the related law.

Attorneys practicing corporate law may be interested in information on mergers or acquisitions. The *Wall Street Journal* database (WSJ) contains this information. In order to find information about the merger of Lucky and Albertson stores, for example, perform the following steps:

1. Access the *Wall Street Journal* database (WSJ).

2. Type the following information in the query box:

   lucky /p albertson

3. The result will be those articles containing those names within the same paragraph.

Corporate financial information is valuable for those firms that have business dealings with these corporations. This material is available in the "Disclosure" database. Suppose you wish to find financial information about General Motors Corporation. Use the following query:

1. Access the DISCLOSURE database.

2. Type the following information in the query box:

   co(general motors)

3. Financial information for General Motors will be found.

THE WESTCLIP SERVICE

The WestClip service enables you to keep up to date on current events and legal developments that affect your practice area of law. You may run a Terms & Connectors query and receive information from this clipping service on a regular basis. The results of the search are delivered to you automatically. In order to activate this service, perform the following steps:

ct "WestClip Directory" from the drop-down list at the top of
age and click "Go."

right frame will show an overview of WestClip.

"Entry Wizard" in the left frame on your screen.

vizard will help you create a new entry.

lready formulated a Terms & Connectors query, perform the
ps:

1. Select "Add to WestClip" from the drop-down list and click "Go."
2. The query is added to the Entry Wizard.
3. Follow the instructions in the wizard to select a frequency setting, next run date, delivery format and destination, and name for the entry.
4. Click "Finish."

UPDATING USING KEYCITE

Recall the many hours spent updating cases using books, and you will appreciate the new Westlaw feature called KeyCite, which is one of the most current, comprehensive, accurate, and easy-to-use citation updating systems. KeyCite allows you to automatically monitor changes in cases and statutes in which you are interested merely by clicking your mouse. It integrates all case law on Westlaw and enables you to trace the history of a case, retrieve a list of all cases citing that case, track legal issues in a case, and find case discussions by legal experts.

KeyCite covers all federal and state cases in West's reporter systems, along with more than one million unpublished cases and over 600 law reviews. Federal case history begins with the earliest reported cases in 1754. State case history begins with 1879. It also includes thousands of *American Jurisprudence 2d* articles, *Couch on Insurance,* Merten's *Law of Federal Taxation, Norton on Bankruptcy Law and Practice 2d,* Rutter Group publications, Witkin's *California Law* materials, and Wright and Miller's *Federal Practice and Procedure.*

Evaluating Case Law

A considerable amount of time and effort needs to be spent in the evaluation of case law in order to determine the following:

1. Is the case "good law"?
2. What is the history of the case?
3. Which other cases have cited this case?
4. What are the relevant legal issues in this case?
5. Which other cases deal with these issues?
6. What other relevant material supports the cited cases?
7. Which other cases are cited by this case?
8. Are all the cited cases that have cited this case "good law"?

Updating Cases with Books

Citator books may have several volumes and monthly supplements that are very expensive. Maintenance is cumbersome and tedious. In order to update a case or statute, several volumes of the books must be reviewed, a process that can take several hours of your time. Yet, information is only as current as your last updated volume, which may be up to a month old.

Cases and statutes are listed by citation only without the case names. The following process is used:

1. Review the citation for the case or statute you are updating.
2. Find the appropriate volume of the citator for your case or statute.
3. Look up the citation and review all subsequent citations listed.
4. If you are updating to find whether the case is "good law" (that is, whether it has been overruled), look for that code below the main case.
5. Find the case or statute that overrules yours.
6. Check all subsequent volumes of the citator series; perform steps 1 through 5 for each supplement.
7. Note the date of the latest supplement. Any cases decided after that date will not appear.

Updating Cases with KeyCite

Access to KeyCite may be obtained by any one of the following methods:

1. Using the Westlaw pull-down menu.
2. Clicking the graphic KC icon in your Westlaw tool bar.
3. Clicking on a status flag, described below, from a case display on Westlaw.
4. If you are in a headnote on Westlaw, clicking on "KeyCite this headnote."

See number 1 in Figure 10-23 for Accessing KeyCite. Numbers 2, 3, 4, and 5 itemize other features of KeyCite.

Special Features of KeyCite

A number of unique features are found within the KeyCite system. Case histories are available within KeyCite the same day they appear in Westlaw.

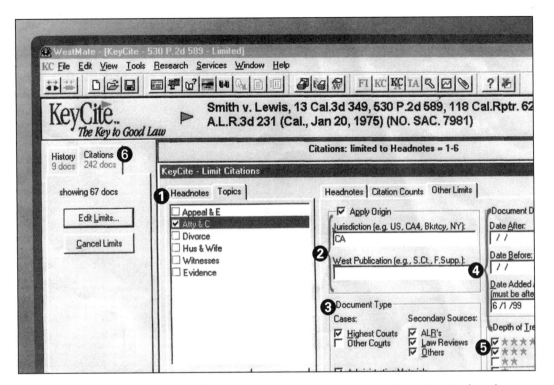

FIGURE 10-23   Accessing KeyCite. Reprinted with permission from *KeyCite* brochure
© 1999 West Group.

Each citing case links the headnotes of all cases referenced within them
using topics and key numbers. A unique graphical display enables you to
find information quickly.

A system using red and yellow flags enables you to quickly determine
any negative history about the case. The red flag means that the case is no
longer "good law" because it has been overruled, reversed, vacated, or ab-
rogated. The yellow flag means the case has some negative history, but it
has not been overruled or reversed. The presence of a blue "H" means that
the case has some history. All of these flags are linked to the appropriate
case citations as soon as the case appears on Westlaw.

A red flag accompaniment to a statute means it has been either amended
or repealed. A yellow flag means there is pending legislation that may
affect a Federal statute.

Green stars show which cases discuss the instant case the most so the
reader can focus on what later courts have said. Starting with those cases
with the most stars enables you to learn the most about a case in the least

amount of time. Figure 10-24 shows the definitions of the different numbers of green stars.

One may think of the stars as being analogous to the positive history of the case and the flags to the negative history. Look at Figure 10-23. Note the red flag at the top of the page under number 2. The researcher should investigate the cited case for negative history.

Now look under number 4 and find the green stars after the case citations. Turn to Figure 10-24 to determine what that number of stars means.

Depth of Treatment Categories		
Examined	★★★★	The citing case contains an extended discussion of the cited case, usually more than a printed page of text.
Discussed	★★★	The citing case contains a substantial discussion of the cited case, usually more than a paragraph but less than a printed page.
Cited	★★	The citing case contains some discussion of the cited case, usually less than a paragraph.
Mentioned	★	The citing case contains a brief reference to the cited case, usually in a string citation.

FIGURE 10-24 Definitions of Green Stars in KeyCite. Reprinted with permission from *KeyCite* brochure © 1999 West Group.

Customizing the KeyCite Display

The KeyCite system has a method for restricting your research. Look at number 3 in Figure 10-23. You may select the full history of the case, only the negative history, or omit the minor history.

Suppose you are about to file an appellate brief with the court. The brief contains many case citations and it must be submitted to the court today. You would likely wish to check only negative history for each case cited in your brief.

Note that all case names are shown in their entirety. Both the name of the case and its citation are displayed.

Key Numbering System

The West key numbering system has been fully integrated into the KeyCite system, hence the word "Key" in its name. Citations may be displayed by both topic and West key number for your own jurisdiction. After you find the proper key number for your case or issue, you can be assured that all relevant cases will be displayed.

Headnotes

Once you find the appropriate headnote topic, you can obtain the full text of the headnote in each relevant case by merely clicking your mouse. Figure 10-25 shows a KeyCite page using a headnote search.

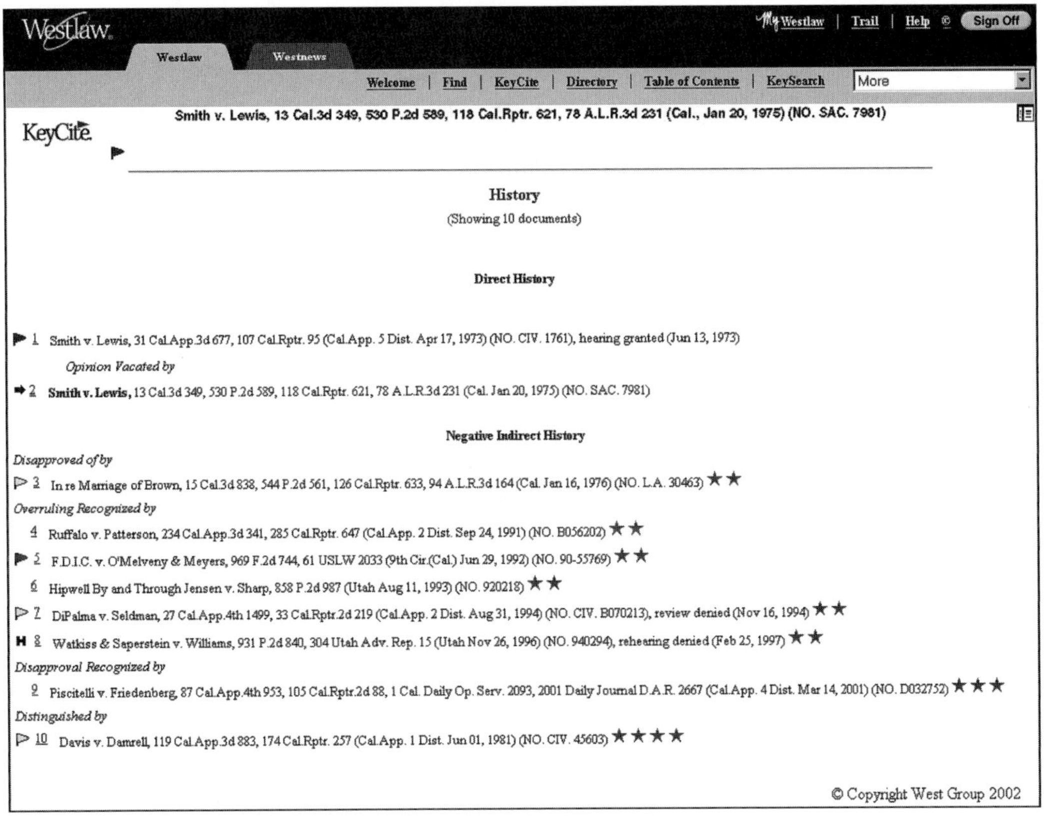

FIGURE 10-25   KeyCite Page using Headnote. Reprinted with permission from **Westlaw.com** © 2002 West Group.

Viewing a KeyCite Case History

Once you find the case in which you are interested in the KeyCite system, the history of the case will be displayed. It is divided into the following sections:

1. *Direct history*—This section traces the history of the case through the appellate process and includes prior and subsequent history.

2. *Negative indirect history*—This section lists cases outside the direct appellate line that might have a negative impact on the instant case.

3. *Related references*—This section lists cases involving the same parties and facts as your case, including those with different legal issues.

Viewing Case Citations

Once you have access to the KeyCite display for your particular case, you can view all cases and secondary sources that cite your case. Click "Citations to the Case" in the left frame of the History of the Case display. A list of citations will be given.

Negative cases that cited your case are listed first. All other cases citing your case follow, categorized by the depth of treatment they give your case. The star system just discussed indicates the depth of treatment.

Number 1 in Figure 10-26 shows the headnote topics available for the search including their key numbers. Click the box or boxes that display the point(s) of law in which you are interested. After you click "OK," the list of citations relevant to that topic will appear.

Note the list of headnote numbers listed under number 2. The underlined blue numbers represent hyperlinks that enable you to conduct a digest search of that particular issue. Number 3 shows the exact wording of the headnote, and number 4 shows how many cases discuss this legal issue.

Limiting Research

Figure 10-26 shows the screen that appears if you click "Other Limits" in KeyCite. Several different limitations are possible to further restrict the information you are seeking.

Following are the restrictions available as noted in numbers 1 through 6 in Figure 10-26:

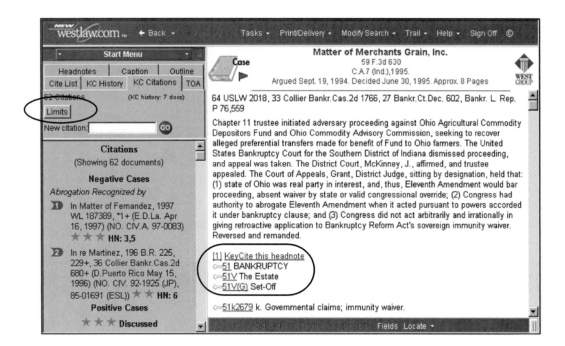

FIGURE 10-26 Limitations in KeyCite. Reprinted with permission from *Discovering Westlaw* © 2000 West Group.

1. You can restrict your search to either headnotes or topics by clicking the appropriate box. In this particular case, the researcher is interested in the topic "Attorney and Client."

2. A particular jurisdiction or West publication provides a further limitation. In this case, the researcher is interested in California materials only.

3. The type of document in which you are interested should be checked under this section. This researcher is interested in opinions of the highest courts as well as many secondary sources.

4. By using the document dates field, the search may be restricted to a specific time period.

5. Note the green star system discussed earlier. Checking the green star boxes limits the search to the most relevant cases.

6. If you wish to know how often this case was cited as well as the average number of citations from the same year and jurisdiction, check this box. In this case, 67 out of 242 documents cited the subject case.

Creating a Table of Authorities

With the mere click of a mouse, a table of authorities may be created for each case in which you are interested. This service provides a list of every case cited within the subject case and includes the following graphical aids:

1. Green stars showing the depth of treatment for the case
2. Red and yellow status flags showing the cases' subsequent negative history

The table of authorities service is useful for finding all cases related to your case. It also provides a valuable tool for doing research into the opposing party's case to help determine any hidden weaknesses. See Figure 10-27 for a Table of Authorities page.

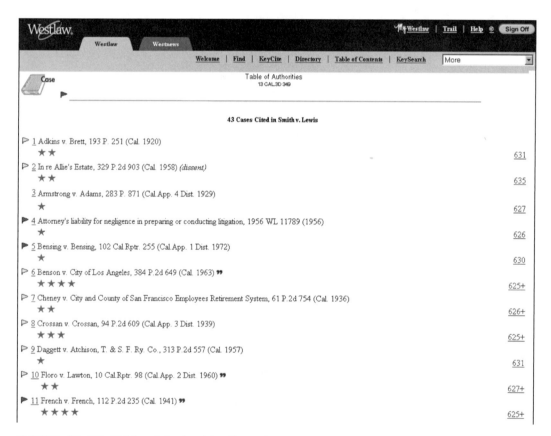

FIGURE 10-27 Table of Authorities Page from KeyCite. Reprinted with permission from **Westlaw.com** © 2002 West Group.

<u>12</u> Hill v. Matthews Paint Co., 308 P.2d 865 (Cal.App. 2 Dist. 1957)

    ★   <u>628</u>

▶ <u>13</u> People v. Ibarra, 386 P.2d 487 (Cal. 1963)

    ★ ★   <u>626</u>

<u>14</u> Kinsey v. Kinsey, 41 Cal.Rptr. 802 (Cal.App. 2 Dist. 1964) *(dissent)*

    ★ ★   <u>635+</u>

▷ <u>15</u> Laird v. T. W. Mather, Inc., 331 P.2d 617 (Cal. 1958)

    ★   <u>631</u>

<u>16</u> Lally v. Kuster, 171 P. 961 (Cal. 1918)

    ★ ★   <u>627+</u>

▷ <u>17</u> In re Lances' Estate, 14 P.2d 768 (Cal. 1932)

    ★   <u>631</u>

<u>18</u> Land v. Gregory, 335 P.2d 141 (Cal.App. 4 Dist. 1959)

    ★   <u>628+</u>

▷ <u>19</u> Lucas v. Hamm, 364 P.2d 685 (Cal. 1961) 🙶

    ★ ★ ★ ★   <u>625+</u>

<u>20</u> In re Manley's Estate, 337 P.2d 487 (Cal.App. 4 Dist. 1959)

    ★   <u>626</u>

▶ <u>21</u> In re Marriage of Fithian, 517 P.2d 449 (Cal. 1974) 🙶

    ★ ★ ★ ★   <u>624+</u>

▶ <u>22</u> In re Marriage of Karlin, 101 Cal.Rptr. 240 (Cal.App. 4 Dist. 1972)

    ★   <u>630</u>

<u>23</u> In re Marriage of Wilson, 519 P.2d 165 (Cal. 1974)

    ★ ★   <u>626+</u>

<u>24</u> Miller v. Superior Court of Los Angeles County, 442 P.2d 663 (Cal. 1968) *(dissent)*

    ★ ★   <u>634</u>

▷ <u>25</u> Nestle v. City of Santa Monica, 496 P.2d 480 (Cal. 1972)

    ★ ★   <u>628+</u>

▷ <u>26</u> Ogle v. Heim, 442 P.2d 659 (Cal. 1968) *(dissent)*

    ★ ★   <u>634+</u>

▷ <u>27</u> Packer v. Board of Retirement of Los Angeles County Peace Officers' Retirement System, 217 P.2d 660 (Cal. 1950) *(dissent)* 🙶

    ★ ★   <u>634</u>

<u>28</u> In re Perryman's Estate, 283 P.2d 298 (Cal.App. 1 Dist. 1955)

    ★   <u>626</u>

▷ <u>29</u> Pete v. Henderson, 269 P.2d 78 (Cal.App. 1 Dist. 1954)

    ★ ★   <u>629</u>

▶ <u>30</u> Phillipson v. Board of Administration, 473 P.2d 765 (Cal. 1970)

    ★ ★ ★   <u>624+</u>

▷ <u>31</u> People v. Pierce, 75 Cal.Rptr. 257 (Cal.App. 3 Dist. 1969)

    ★   <u>631</u>

<u>32</u> Pineda v. Craven, 424 F.2d 369 (9th Cir.(Cal.) 1970) 🙶

    ★ ★   <u>627</u>

▷ <u>33</u> Primm v. Primm, 299 P.2d 231 (Cal. 1956)

    ★   <u>629</u>

▷ <u>34</u> See v. See, 415 P.2d 776 (Cal. 1966) *(dissent)*

    ★ ★   <u>636</u>

<u>35</u> Singh v. Frye, 2 Cal.Rptr. 372 (Cal.App. 3 Dist. 1960) *(dissent)*

    ★ ★   <u>632</u>

<u>36</u> Sprague v. Morgan, 8 Cal.Rptr. 347 (Cal.App. 1 Dist. 1960) 🙶

    ★ ★ ★   <u>626+</u>

FIGURE 10-27   *(continued)*

<u>37</u> Thomas v. Thomas, 13 Cal.Rptr. 872 (Cal.App. 2 Dist. 1961) *(dissent)*
   ★ ★   <u>634</u>

   <u>38</u> Valdez v. Clark, 343 P.2d 281 (Cal.App. 2 Dist. 1959)
   ★ ★   <u>628</u>

▶ <u>39</u> Waite v. Waite, 492 P.2d 13 (Cal. 1972)
   ★ ★ ★   <u>624+</u>

▷ <u>40</u> People v. Watson, 299 P.2d 243 (Cal. 1956)
   ★   <u>632</u>

▶ <u>41</u> Williamson v. Williamson, 21 Cal.Rptr. 164 (Cal.App. 2 Dist. 1962)
   ★ ★ ★   <u>625+</u>

▶ <u>42</u> Wissner v. Wissner, 201 P.2d 837 (Cal.App. 3 Dist. 1949) *(dissent)*
   ★ ★   <u>635</u>

▷ <u>43</u> Wissner v. Wissner, 70 S.Ct. 398 (U.S.Cal. 1950) *(dissent)*
   ★ ★   <u>635+</u>

FIGURE 10-27 *(continued)*

KeyCite Alert

A recent addition to the KeyCite system is a tracking device for keeping you informed of important developments that affect relevant cases and statutes. The KeyCite Alert informs you automatically of any changes or updates in the particular area of interest. Limits can be made based on:

1. Negative history (the red and yellow flag system)
2. Treatment depth (the green star system)
3. Headnotes or legal issues
4. Specific jurisdictions
5. Notes of decisions
6. Time limits

See Figure 10-28 for a KeyCite Alert system entry using the following descriptions:

1. Citation
2. Type of history
3. Frequency option
4. Timing
5. Place of delivery
6. Full-text option

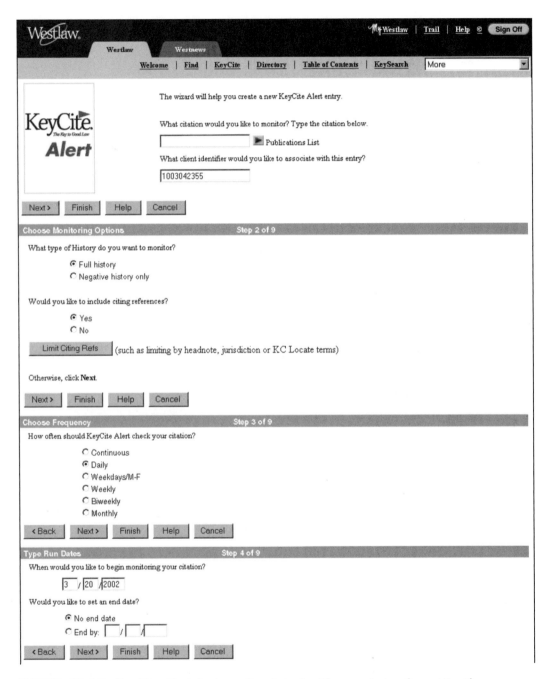

FIGURE 10-28 KeyCite Alert System. Reprinted with permission from **Westlaw.com** © 2002 West Group.

Choose Destination   Step 5 of 9

Where would you like the results delivered?

    ○ Attached Printer
    ○ Download to Disk
    ○ Save
    ○ Fax Machine
    ● E-mail

| < Back | Next > | Finish | Help | Cancel |

Type E-mail Address(es)   Step 6 of 9

You may choose multiple delivery locations.

To what e-mail address(es) would you like your results delivered? (separate with semicolons)

[   ]

Wireless address(es): (separate with semicolons)

[   ]

☑ Include summary information with KeyCite Alert results.

| < Back | Next > | Finish | Help | Cancel |

Choose Full Text Options   Step 7 of 9

Would you like the full text of alerted documents?

    ○ Yes
    ● No

Note: Each full text document retrieved may be separately billed according to your price plan.

| < Back | Next > | Finish | Help | Cancel |

Type Notes   Step 8 of 9

Would you like to make any notes about your entry?

[   ]

| < Back | Next > | Finish | Help | Cancel |

Confirm Settings   Step 9 of 9

Your entry has the following settings:

    Citation: 13 Cal.3d 349
    Client Identifier: 1003042355
    History: Full History
    Citing References: On
    Frequency: Daily
    Next Run Date: 03/20/2002
    End Date: None
    Delivery: E-mail
    Full Text: Off
    Notes: << none >>

Click **Finish** to save your entry.

| < Back | Finish | Help | Cancel |

FIGURE 10-28   *(continued)*

STARTING WESTLAW THROUGH WESTMATE———————

Prior to beginning your research session, you must establish a connection to Westlaw. The following steps indicate the proper procedure:

1. Click the "Start" button.
2. Make the following choices:
   a. Choose "Programs"
   b. Choose "West Applications"
   c. Choose "WESTMATE."
3. You will see the dialog box for signing on to Westlaw. Type your password and client ID into the boxes provided for that purpose.
4. Select a dialing location from the drop-down list entitled "My Location" if you are using a local modem.
5. Check the appropriate billing method, either hourly or transactional.
6. Click "OK."
7. The "Welcome to Westlaw" screen will appear.

In order to sign off Westlaw from the Westmate software, perform the following steps:

1. Find the File menu and choose "Sign off Westlaw."
2. Click the proper button if you wish to save the current project on which you are working.
3. You will see the Westlaw Time Summary box that indicates how much time you have been online with Westlaw. You are not yet disconnected from the system.
4. Click "OK."
5. To exit from Westmate, choose "Exit" from your File menu.

Customizing Westmate

Westmate provides the capability to make changes in the system to customize its use for your own particular needs. You can change your documents display, the text type, fonts, and color of text, and your file storage.

To change how items appear on your screen, choose "Options" from the Tools menu. Star paging display options enable you to display pagination from printed publications obtained on Westlaw.

To change the text type, font, font size, and color of text in documents, choose "Fonts" from "Options" in the Tools menu. To change the location for storage of your files—that is, to choose a different download folder—click "File Locations" from "Options." A dialog box will appear. You may also save specific queries and actions in a separate project folder.

Communications Options

With the use of the Westmate software, you may set up communications options for accessing Westlaw, specify sign-on options, and modify advanced communications access. Most people will, however, find the default settings that have already been provided with the system satisfactory.

If you are using a local modem, you will set up the general communications from "Communications Options" in the Tools menu. The page will display a drop-down list of modems or other communications devices, such as Internet TCP/IP or Eicon. Select your modem from the list.

Accessing Westmate from Another Location

There may be occasions when you are not dialing from your present location. In order to access Westlaw from another place, click "Dialing Properties" in the Communications Setup—General dialog box. Select the number and area code as well as any numbers that must be dialed to access an outside line. Clicking "Phone Numbers" from "Communications Options" will enable you to determine the current access phone numbers.

In order to add a telephone number, click "Next" and specify your current location. Click "Next" and you will be able to retrieve telephone numbers for your current location.

USING WESTMATE

After you have installed Westmate on your computer, you will notice an icon for Westmate on your desktop. Double-click on this icon to enter the Westlaw system.

You will notice a "Tip of the Day" box giving you a hint on how to use a particular function. Click "Close" to access the "Sign on to Westlaw" screen. Type in your password and client identifier and click "OK." You will be taken to the "Welcome to Westlaw" display.

The research principles used with Westmate are the same as those used when you are accessing Westlaw via the Internet. Many of the Web pages look the same. The "Welcome to Westlaw" window enables you to start the following tasks by choosing items:

1. Click your right mouse button; choose an item from the pop-up menu.
2. Select the drop-down menu; choose an item from it.
3. Click one of the buttons on the left side of the window to
   a. Search for a database.
   b. Display a customized list of databases.
   c. Verify with KeyCite.
   d. Find a document by citation.
   e. Display your saved queries in the WestClip directory.
   f. Search for a key number and topic using the key numbering system.
4. If you know the identifier for the database, type it in the "Database" window and click "Search."

Main Button Toolbar

Most Westmate windows display a button toolbar at the top of the screen. The buttons and their functions are given in Figure 10-29 on page 178. If the toolbar is displayed on the screen, you can click on one of the buttons to perform the described function.

Bookmarks

You may already be familiar with bookmarks, a feature that allows you to mark favorite Web sites to which you wish to return frequently. This feature is also available in the Westmate system so that you can store the databases or services that you use most often. Use one of the following methods to access it:

1. Click "Favorite Places" from the list that appears when you click your right mouse button.
2. Access the "Research" Menu and click "Favorite Places."

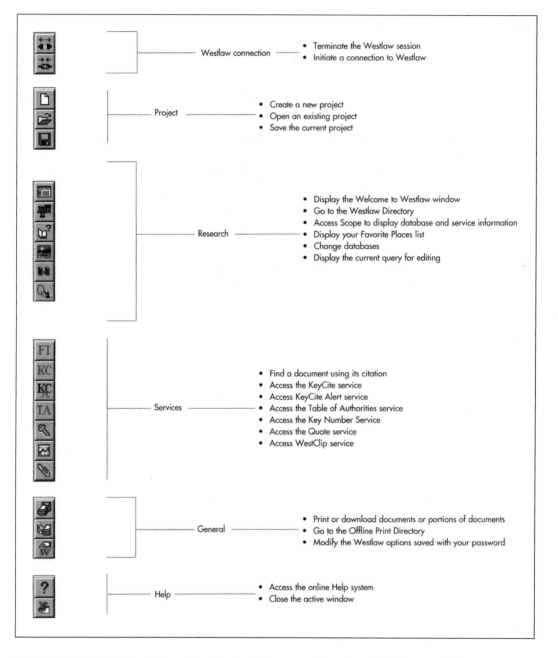

FIGURE 10-29 Main Button Toolbar in Westmate. Reprinted with permission from *Using WestMate for Windows 95 and Windows NT* © 1999 West Group.

3. From the "Welcome to Westlaw" screen, choose "Favorite Places" from the left side of the screen.

4. From the Main Menu page, choose "Favorite Places" from the buttons displayed.

Once the list for Favorite Places is displayed on your screen, you may add the database to your list, choose a list from the list of state or practice-area templates, or find databases to add to the list from those listed in the Westlaw Directory.

Westlaw Directory

The Westlaw Directory provides a list of all Westlaw services and databases in the form of an index. This directory may be accessed in three different ways:

1. In the "Research" menu, choose "Westlaw Directory."

2. On the Main Screen, click on the "Westlaw Directory" button.

3. On the "Welcome to Westlaw" page, click on the "Choose a Database" button on the left side of the screen.

Once you have accessed the directory, the icons on the left side of the list enable you to view its subsections. Click an icon for a list of subsections. Figure 10-30 on page 180 shows an example of the Westlaw Directory and the subdirectory for Federal Materials.

Note that the "Scope" option is available from Westmate. This option enables you to see the specific features of the particular database or service. "Scope" can be accessed in one of the following ways:

1. Click "Scope" from the pop-up menu that appears when you click your right mouse button.

2. Note the buttons on the main page and click "Scope."

To exit the Scope feature, click the button to close the window that is located in the upper-right corner of the window.

Retrieving Documents by Citation

You may retrieve documents by using their citation with the "Find" feature. In order to access "Find," perform one of the following steps:

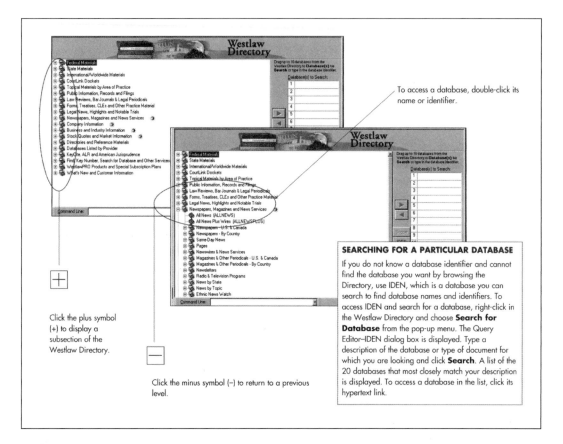

FIGURE 10-30 Westlaw Directory Using Westmate. Reprinted with permission from *Using WestMate for Windows 95 and Windows NT* © 1999 West Group.

1. From the "Welcome to Westlaw" page, click "Find a Document" on the left side of the screen.

2. From the Main Page, click "Find a Document" from the button bar.

3. Choose "Find a Document" from the list that appears when you click your right mouse button.

4. Click "Find a Document" from the "Research" menu.

Once you are on the "Find" page, the methods for finding documents are similar to those described earlier. Type your citation in the text box and click "OK."

Documents that may be retrieved with the "Find" feature include federal and state statutes, federal and state case law, administrative decisions, law reviews, legal periodicals, and news items. Some examples of retrievable items and their citations follow:

United States Supreme Court cases	215 sct 1133
Federal Rules of Evidence	fre 333
Article from *Time Magazine*	3/6/99 timemag 11
Harvard Law Review Article	32 harv l rev 366

Conducting Searches

A detailed description of how to find documents using a Natural Language or Terms & Connectors search was presented earlier in this chapter. The same methods are used with Westmate.

Surveying Documents

Once you have conducted a search, the case or other document will appear on your screen. The right mouse button may be used to perform the following functions:

1. Move between pages of the document.
2. Go to a list of documents found.
3. Edit your original query.
4. Locate the point at which particular terms appear in the document.
5. Send the document to a printer or disk to be copied.
6. Update the document appearing on the screen.

Figure 10-31 on page 182 shows a Westmate page after a search has been conducted, with the pop-up menu that appears when you click the right mouse button appearing on the right side of the screen.

Note the toolbar or pull-down menu at the top of the screen display. The arrow keys can be used to move to the "Previous" or "Next" search term or document. Other functions are explained within the toolbar itself.

The title of the window at the top of the screen indicates the database that was searched, as well as the description you used to find the document indicated. Note the large arrow in the middle of the screen. This indicates that negative or positive history will be available in the KeyCite system, as described earlier. Hypertext links are available at the bottom of the page for purposes of moving to other locations in Westlaw. If you click the

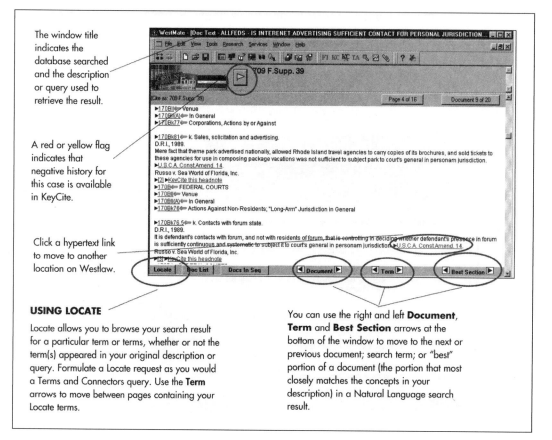

The window title indicates the database searched and the description or query used to retrieve the result.

A red or yellow flag indicates that negative history for this case is available in KeyCite.

Click a hypertext link to move to another location on Westlaw.

USING LOCATE

Locate allows you to browse your search result for a particular term or terms, whether or not the term(s) appeared in your original description or query. Formulate a Locate request as you would a Terms and Connectors query. Use the **Term** arrows to move between pages containing your Locate terms.

You can use the right and left **Document**, **Term** and **Best Section** arrows at the bottom of the window to move to the next or previous document; search term; or "best" portion of a document (the portion that most closely matches the concepts in your description) in a Natural Language search result.

FIGURE 10-31   Document Window Display. Reprinted with permission from *Using WestMate for Windows 95 and Windows NT* © 1999 West Group.

"Page" or "Document" box on the bottom of the screen, you will be able to immediately go to a specific page or document.

Viewing a List of Citations

The method used for viewing a list of citations obtained from your particular search is the same as that described under "Surveying Documents." Once again, the right mouse button may be used to perform functions.

If you click your right mouse button, you will see a list from which you can choose the following functions:

1. See the full document.

2. See a summary of your search result.

3. Locate items within the documents.
4. Print or download items.
5. Change the order in which documents are shown.

Organizing Projects

One major advantage of using Westmate is the ability to organize your research sessions into folders for future use. Each research session is stored in an electronic folder called a "project" that can be accessed at a later date. These projects can be separated by client identifier. Projects are stored in a "Project Log" that is accessed by choosing "Project" from the "View" menu.

Saving Projects

Before you sign off Westlaw, you should either choose "Save Project" from the File menu or click the button titled "Save Project" on the main button toolbar. Just as you save files on your computer, you would then type an identification into the File Name box. Up to eight characters can be used. Click "Save," and the project will be saved to the project file unless you specify another directory in which you would like your project placed.

Each time you sign on to Westlaw using Westmate, new projects are created automatically. But suppose you have completed one project and wish to start another one without having to sign off Westlaw and then sign back on again. You may start a new project during a current session as follows:

1. Go to the File menu.
2. Click on "New Project."

You may click "New Project" on the main button toolbar to perform this function.

If the previous project has not been saved, you will be reminded to save it. The "New Project" dialog box will be displayed. Enter the new project number or client identifier into the box and click "OK."

Opening Saved Projects

The main button toolbar has a button called "Open Project." Clicking on this button will display a list of all previously created projects. Click on the one you wish to open. Alternatively, you can also open existing projects from the File menu by clicking "Open Project" there.

Printing and Downloading

Various methods are available for printing or copying to a diskette or another location. You may print documents on an attached printer, download it to disk, download it to an e-mail, download it to a fax machine, save it on Westlaw, send it to a stand-alone printer, or send it to Westprint for mailing. Note that all users may not have all of these options.

The following steps are required:

1. With the document on your page, click the right mouse button and choose "Send to Destination" from the menu. Or you may click the "File" menu and choose "Send to Destination." A third method is to choose "Select a Destination" from the main button toolbar.

2. Select the destination from the list given.

3. Choose the options desired from the dialog box on your screen.

Signing Off

To sign off Westmate, you must first sign off Westlaw. Exit from Westmate in the following manner:

1. Either choose "Sign Off Westlaw" from your File menu, or click the button for "Sign Off Westlaw" on your main button toolbar.

2. Choose "Exit" from the Westmate file menu.

Additional Westmate Functions

Note that all functions available using Westmate have not been discussed. Those that are the same as those used when you access Westlaw from the Internet are described earlier.

SUMMARY

A subscription to Westlaw must be obtained in order to use the service. The new system provides tabs to view pertinent information without leaving the original document on your screen. The screen image looks like a book page.

The system enables you to conduct word searches. Cases may be updated by using KeyCite. Access to Westlaw is provided either via special software known as Westmate or by using a password and client identifier on the Internet. This chapter provides a comprehensive description of the Westlaw system and how to use it.

REVIEW QUESTIONS

1. What are the advantages of using the Westlaw system?
2. Describe the new Westlaw system.
3. What are the Web addresses for accessing Westlaw on the Internet?
4. How is a subscription to Westlaw obtained?
5. Under what circumstances would you use the KeyCite system? Give an example.

PRACTICAL PROBLEMS
(if you have access to Westlaw)

1. Find the statutes for your state. Does your state allow capital punishment? What did you key (type) into the query box to get this information?
2. Your client has been accused of racketeering. The attorney has asked you to find the federal statute dealing with this topic and outline the circumstances under which an individual can be charged with the crime. The client has been arrested for drug trafficking in another state.
3. A client has been suspended from high school for wearing inappropriate clothing at school. Specifically, the student wore a T-shirt with what the school called "obscene language" written on it. Can a public institution in your state require a dress code of students? Was the suspension valid in your state?

PRACTICAL PROBLEMS (without access to Westlaw)

1. Describe the procedures you would follow in problem 1 above to find the statutes for your state.
2. Frame an issue statement using WIN to answer the following question: Can a homeless person solicit funds at a public shopping mall?
3. Using a Digest Field search, list the steps you would follow to conduct a search to answer the question in problem 2.

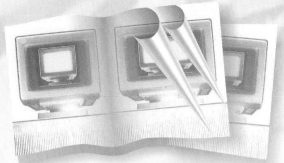

CHAPTER 11

Using LEXIS

INTRODUCTION

The LEXIS® system was first introduced to the public in 1973. It has been a leading example of computerized legal research since that time. This system is used by attorneys in many states and countries, and a number of colleges and law schools incorporate the study of LEXIS into their legal research classes. LEXIS is available as an online subscription service.

LEXIS is organized into "libraries" for broad categories of material and into "files" for more specific categories. For example, the General Federal (GENFED) "library" divides the federal sources into "files" of primary and secondary authorities.

Suppose you were searching for a federal district court case for New York. You would access the GENFED library and then the DIST file for federal district court opinions. A further subfile would include the different state cases and opinions. Think of the GENFED library as a file drawer with the narrower federal categories as separate folders within that drawer.

Searching in LEXIS uses the same research techniques described in earlier chapters for Westlaw. However, there are some unique features in the LEXIS system that will be discussed here.

SEARCHING IN LEXIS

Key word searches are similar to those conducted in Westlaw. When framing an issue statement to be searched, be as specific as possible. Using a general word such as "negligence" will, for instance, provide thousands of responses that may not be pertinent to the case at hand. In searching for a specific phrase, enclose the phrase in quotation marks, such as "drunk driving" or "driving under the influence."

Unique Features

Irregular Plural Forms   LEXIS automatically searches for the standard plural and possessive forms of a word. However, if the word has an irregular plural form, such as children, you should search for both using the connector "or." For example, your query would read "child or children."

Spelling   Although LEXIS will automatically search for obvious alternative spellings, such as 3d and 3rd for third, it may not recognize variations of all spellings. Additionally, some authors may accidentally misspell a critical word. If the misspelled word is actually a legitimate spelling, the system cannot recognize it as an error. Therefore, try to anticipate alternative spellings of the word and use both spellings in the search. If you see that the author has used two different spellings for the same word, adapt your search to include multiple spellings.

Additional Typed Characters   The chart in Figure 11-1 shows additional characters and their uses in LEXIS. When typing words into your search, treat a hyphen as a space between the words. In other words, treat a hyphenated word as two separate words.

Other less common abbreviations used in LEXIS are available in the materials provided to subscribers.

FINDING STATUTES

Statutory law includes all statutes enacted by legislatures. Often the interpretation of the statutory language is dependent upon the original intent of the legislature. Therefore, in addition to finding the statute itself, it is usually necessary to research the legislative history and later case interpretations of the statute by the judiciary to clarify the legislature's intent.

Federal Statutes by Citation

In order to find a federal statute in LEXIS when you know the title and section number, you can use the LEXSTAT feature. For example, if you

!	Searches for variations in the root word. Searches for all words containing the alphabetic characters appearing before the "!". Example: "**administ!**" retrieves **administer, administrator, administration, administrative.**
*	Searches for words containing any character where the * is indicated. Example: "**wom*n**" retrieves **woman, women;** "**bank*****" retrieves **bank, banking, banker** but not **bankrupt**, which has four letters after the root word.
W/n	A **Connector** that retrieves words found within a specified number ("n") of words of each other. For example: **personal w/2 injury** finds documents with "personal" and "injury" within two words of each other.
AND	Finds documents containing both words no matter how close together or far apart. For example: **personal AND injury** finds all documents containing both words.
OR	Finds documents containing either word. For example: **injury OR harm** retrieves documents containing either of the terms.

FIGURE 11-1 Typed Characters Used in LEXIS

were searching for Section 22 of Title 39 of the United States Code, your query would be:

lexstat 39 usc 22

Federal Statutes by Subject

Find a federal statute by its subject in much the same way you would search for a case. Access the statutes section of LEXIS and type in the topic of the statute. For instance, suppose your client is accused of racketeering. To find the applicable statute, go to the LEXSTAT section of LEXIS and type your query:

racketeering

Legislative History of Federal Statutes

Several sources are available for finding the legislative history of federal statutes. The following publications, available on LEXIS, can be used to find the original intent of the legislature:

1. *United States Code Congressional and Administrative News*—A number of congressional committee reports are contained in the legislative history segment of this publication.

2. *Committee Hearings/Reports*—The LEXIS specialized libraries contain many transcripts of the hearings on certain laws before they were enacted.

3. *Congressional Record*—Searching under the key words or bill number enables you to find the daily report of the debates on the floor of both houses of Congress.

4. *Congressional Information Service*—This service provides an index to congressional publications that aid in finding the legislative history of federal laws.

State Statutes

A majority of state codes may be found on the LEXIS service; however, you should be familiar with the state's numbering system before attempting to find their codes on LEXIS. For example, some states use a numerical system that includes all of their codes, while others use a system comprised of topics and sections. Refer to the indices in the LEXIS system for the proper code words or numbers to use for finding your state's statutes.

FINDING CASES

Using Citation

The LEXSEE feature enables you to find a case if you have its citation. To find the case listed in volume 22, page 425 of the *United States Reports,* you would use the following search terms:

lexsee 22 us 425

Using Case Information

Suppose you were interested in finding the famous *Marvin v. Marvin* case from California that was appealed to the federal courts and the United States Supreme Court. You would frame an issue that included all pertinent information about this case. Your search might include the following:

Marvin AND palimony AND California

plus any other search terms you have about that specific case.

Using Digests

The same limitations that apply to finding cases in digests in a law library are applicable to using these digests for finding cases on LEXIS. Cases in digests are generally categorized under broad legal topics so the researcher must use several key words to find the relevant cases. After finding appropriate cases under the digest topics, try to develop additional, more specific subjects under which to search.

ADMINISTRATIVE LAW SEARCHES

Laws that have been established by the various government agencies are encompassed in administrative law. Each agency establishes its own rules and regulations that must be followed when dealing with that particular agency.

Federal Register

The *Federal Register* contains the initial and final proposals for federal regulations; it is published on a daily basis. Publications in the *Federal Register* may also include supplementary information defining changes that occurred between the initial proposal and the final regulation. The LEXIS service contains the full text of the *Federal Register* since July, 1980.

Code of Federal Regulations

LEXIS publishes the full text of the *Code of Federal Regulations* (*CFR*). All regulations are classified into subject topics (titles) in alphabetical order. It includes over 150 volumes.

Federal Regulations by Topic

A topic search for federal regulations is handled in the same way as a key word search is conducted for cases. You can search the full text of both the *CFR* and the *Federal Register* by using a key word search. If you know the governmental agency that issued the regulation, you can limit your search to the regulations of that agency. For example, to find a regulation issued by the Department of Transportation and related to airline deregulation, you may use the following key words:

agency (transportation) AND airline w/5 deregulation

State Administrative Regulations

Some state regulations are available in the LEXIS service under the LEXIS state libraries. In order to determine whether your state's administrative regulations are found within the service, conduct a search in the state subject-matter library.

FINDING SECONDARY SOURCES

Secondary sources are useful for finding information about primary authority, as well as for researching new and emerging areas of the law. The most widely used sources are legal encyclopedias and legal dictionaries. Searching for the definition of a word in LEXIS is much like any other key word search. Simply search for the word or phrase you wish to have defined.

Legal Treatises

A comprehensive analysis of a particular legal specialty area may be found in various legal treatises. Many of these treatises are available on LEXIS. Some comprise many volumes, while others can be found in a single volume. You can search for a particular series in the LEXIS library, as well as for the topic in which you are interested.

Periodicals

A number of legal periodicals are available. Included are bar journals, legal newspapers, law reviews, and legal newsletters, most of which are found in the Law Review (LAW.REV) library and the LEXIS/NEXIS libraries. Publications in the administrative law area may be covered in the NEXIS service publications.

Case Annotations

Some reports are heavily annotated with references to Law Review articles and editors' analyses of points of law covered in the cases. Of particular significance are the American Law Reports (ALR) and the United States Supreme Court Reports, Lawyers' Edition (L.Ed.), both of which are available on the LEXIS service.

In order to find only annotations in the ALR, you can initiate a search under the **ANNO** file; to find both cases and annotations, use **GENFED COURTS** or **STATES OMNI**.

GENERAL INFORMATION

A unique feature of the LEXIS service is the companion NEXIS feature that provides a vast amount of information from many nonlegal sources. For instance, newspapers from throughout the country often provide information on case settlements in which an attorney is involved. News articles can be found about cases involving opposing counsel or the judge in a particular case. Searches in NEXIS are conducted the same as in LEXIS: Either find the particular periodical in which you are interested, or conduct a key word search for the topic of interest.

Over 350 general business and news sources are available in NEXIS. General newspapers and trade journals can be found, as well as information about prospective clients and opposing counsel. It is even possible to locate expert witnesses by using NEXIS.

Shepard's Citations

Once you have found a pertinent case or statute, the next step is determining whether this information is still valid. Shepard's Citation Service is used to establish whether the case has been overruled or the statute has been repealed. *Shepard's* is the most extensively used citator service.

Using the hard copy version of *Shepard's* is cumbersome. You must check each volume of *Shepard's* and carefully review each time period since the subject case or statute was instituted. There may be hard copies, soft copies, updates, and advance sheets to evaluate.

However, "Shepardizing" on LEXIS can be instantaneous and involves merely transmitting the citation preceded by the word "shep." For example, to find 11 Cal.2d 255, key in the following request:

shep 11 cal.2d 255

If you are reading a case on LEXIS and wish to Shepardize it, just key in

shep

and that case will be instantly Shepardized.

When the results of the Shepardized case are transmitted, each case is numbered. In order to view one of the numbered cases, just key in the number and the case will appear on the screen. To return to the list of cases, key in

resume shep

AUTO-CITE

An online citation service of LEXIS provides some different information from *Shepard's*. It is a valuable tool in checking the accuracy of the typed citation and the spellings in the case name. It is also useful for determining whether the case decision is still valid: that is, is the case still "good law"?

Using the Auto-Cite service and keying in the citation for the case yields the following information about the case:

1. Name
2. Jurisdiction
3. Year of the court decision
4. Parallel citations
5. History of the case (prior and subsequent)
6. Related cases involving the same parties
7. Case citations affecting the case's validity
8. Citations of negative prior decisions
9. *ALR* and *L.Ed.* citations

Accessing Auto-Cite involves placing **ac** before the citation in your query. For example, keying

ac 22 cal.2d 555

will enable you to find the case information just listed at 22 Cal.2d 555.

SPECIALIZED SOURCES

In today's complex society it is imperative that the attorney and paralegal be able to find information about a broad spectrum of specialty fields of the law. LEXIS provides the means to initiate searches on virtually any legal area through its specialized online libraries where both primary and secondary sources are available.

For example, suppose you are representing a hospital in New York. The topic is experimental treatments for terminally ill patients. You can use the Health Law Library in LEXIS to conduct a search as follows:

Go to **HEALTH Library**

Look for file on **NY**

Key in your search request, which might be:

experimental treatments w/10 terminal! ill w/5 patients

All documents containing these key words will be found in the Health Library.

Many other specialty databases are available with LEXIS, including the following:

1. Law and medicine
2. Tax law
3. Securities
4. Corporate law
5. Intellectual property
6. International law
7. Laws of other countries

In order to conduct an inquiry into one of these areas, you must first access the appropriate database and then form your query. For a list of databases, see the database directory on LEXIS.

LEXIS ONLINE

The LEXIS system can be accessed online if you have a subscription to the service. Over 31,000 sources may be found by using the Source Locator. A list of all sources on the system will be displayed if "All" is checked in each classification. However, more definitive results are obtained if the query indicates at least one or two specific categories.

Among the other sources accessible online are pages for practice areas, corporate counsel, public records, law schools, the *Martindale-Hubbell Legal Directory of Attorneys and Law Firms,* paralegal information, the National Fraud Center, and links to other legal sites.

SUMMARY

LEXIS is a leading example of computerized legal research and is used by attorneys and paralegals in many states and countries. It is also available to paralegal programs at a reduced subscription price. Although the same basic research techniques are used in LEXIS and Westlaw, the unique features of the LEXIS system are described in this chapter.

REVIEW QUESTIONS

1. How is LEXIS organized for accessing broad categories of material?
2. What is found in the General Federal library database?
3. What is the code used to find federal district court cases?
4. How do you search for irregular plural forms in LEXIS?
5. What does the "*" character indicate?

PRACTICAL PROBLEMS

1. You have been asked by your employer to prepare a memorandum comparing the advantages and disadvantages of the various computerized legal research systems. Compare the systems, including the subscription and online services, and suggest which system represents the best value.

2. Frame a key word search for the following case:

    The clients are homeowners in a new development built in your community. They have contacted your office, which specializes in construction defects cases, to determine the feasibility of filing a class action lawsuit against the developer. The attorney has asked you to ascertain whether similar cases have been filed against the developer by homeowners in other developments they have built. The developer's name is Bad Builders, Inc. Frame an issue statement for your search.

CHAPTER 12

CD-ROM and Other Research Materials

INTRODUCTION TO CD-ROMs

A CD-ROM of research materials is similar to a music CD; however, these CDs contain data but no sound. One of the major advantages of these research tools is the large volume of information that can be stored on each CD. The equivalent of over 100 volumes of text can be stored on a CD. To access this material you must have a compact disc drive on your computer.

The disadvantage of CD systems is the same as that of books: updating. Once the CD or book is printed, it must be reprinted (updated) in order to make the latest information available. The CD is only as current as the update. Updates require the reissuing of a new disc of current information or an online update, which is a service available from some manufacturers. However, you may save a considerable amount of money by using CDs instead of books or online systems. Books and the capability to access online resources via a modem or Internet connection are costly.

Many legal publications that exist in book form are also available on CD. Imagine how much storage space can be saved by replacing 100 volumes of books with one CD. With office space in larger metropolitan areas becoming more expensive, space is at a premium. It is economically sound to replace a complete law library with one small cabinet of CDs. Unfortunately some of the older books may not be in a machine-readable format and cannot be readily transferred to a CD. As new technology develops, no doubt this problem will be solved.

Many attorneys are replacing large portions of their law libraries with CDs. Some states have their codes and statutes available on CD, with updates published every few months. A significant number of pleadings and forms are available on CD, enabling the paralegal or secretary to insert appropriate information for individual cases by keying directly into the form displayed on the computer monitor.

West Publishing Company has developed a significant number of legal sources in CD format. Their state libraries include statutory and case materials from most states. Federal materials include bankruptcy, government contracts, military justice, federal procedures, federal practice, and federal taxation.

With the use of local area networks (LANs), multiple users can access the same CD-ROM materials. This is a major advantage of using CD-ROMs over the use of the book itself. Only one person can use a book at a time; however, with network technology many people may access the same CD at the same time.

Attorney Directories

A number of directories of attorneys are available on CD. The *Martindale-Hubbell Directory* of all attorneys in the United States may be purchased on CD. Updates are available on a regular basis.

Some states have local directories of their attorneys, as well as of government legal offices, courts, administrative offices, and governmental offices. For instance, California publishes the *Parker Directory* twice a year. It contains one volume of all California lawyers by county, and a second volume of government legal offices and courts, as well as legislative offices and other governmental entities. On paper, *Parker's* occupies two large volumes; on CD, *Parker's* is available as a few CDs. Updates are available every six months.

Treatises

Treatises on many areas of law, including bankruptcy, personal injury, environmental law, immigration, and many other specialty areas are now on CD.

Shepard's Citations

Shepard's has most state cases and statutes available on CD, as well as all of the United States and federal materials. Updates are sent on a monthly basis so that current information is accessible.

American Law Reports

In general, the annotations found in *ALR* are concise, authoritative, and well written. Cases cited include all jurisdictions. *ALR on LawDesk* includes all of the latest annotations of *ALR* on a single CD. An extensive online help system is available with the system. The user may search the text, titles, titles/outlines, citation, or the index.

Searches on CD

Most manufacturers provide search software with their products so that the user can conduct full-text searches to access relevant material. Lists of relevant documents, or the documents themselves, can then be saved and/or printed.

Storage

CD-ROM technology is useful for storage of large amounts of data. Many firms are using CD systems for scanning full texts and images from their cases. Any paper-intensive case lends itself to storage on CDs instead of a computer hard drive or multiple diskettes.

One CD holds approximately 300,000 single-spaced pages. That same number of pages would require 1,500 diskettes. One CD will store 630,000 megabytes of information.

CD-ROMs are conveniently portable, particularly in those situations where the attorney or paralegal is required to transport large amounts of case information to another location, such as to another office or the courts.

Software on CD

Most software manufacturers package their software on CD, often with free demonstration packets that enable you to "try before you buy." You can insert the CD and actually view a demonstration of that software. Generally, the software itself is accessible via a password. The CD may also contain a User's Manual.

As more and better software packages are developed on CD, it is becoming increasingly advantageous to utilize these systems. Some legal professionals believe that books for research are becoming obsolete. Perhaps the law library of the future will be composed of computer terminals and screens, CD libraries that are available to many networked users, and online services.

INTRODUCTION TO LOISLAW

Loislaw® is a relatively new leader in the computer-assisted legal research field. Its Internet and CD-ROM libraries provide access to over ten million documents and provide a complete package of federal and state law. Their aim is to provide low-cost, high-quality legal research capabilities to the legal community.

Both case law and statutory law are available directly from the courts and legislative sources. Electronic advance sheets are usable within 72 hours of their release by the courts. As an extra convenience for users of the Internet, new cases are automatically integrated into the case law databases, eliminating the necessity of searching the existing cases and new cases separately. CD-ROM users are provided with weekly electronic advance sheets, which are directly downloadable to their PC.

Loislaw has its own method of updating documents called GlobalCite^{SM}, which shows a list of all Loislaw documents in which the subject document is cited. It also provides the capability of using its system on a PC network so that several users can access the system simultaneously without incurring additional charges.

Several differently priced service plans are provided. For instance, the state and federal collection, Option One, combines the state law library and the federal circuit court decisions for your state, as well as the United States Reports, United States Supreme Court Rules, and the United States Code. A full price list for all Loislaw services is available on their Web page at:

http://www.loislaw.com

See Figure 12-1 for the Loislaw home page. A summary of the services available in Loislaw is found in Figures 12-2 and 12-3 on pages 204 and 205.

FIGURE 12-1 Loislaw Home Page. Reprinted with permission from **Loislaw.com**
© 2001 Loislaw.com, Inc., An Aspen Publishers Company.

Two features included in all Professional Library subscriptions at no cost are GlobalCite, the citation research service, and LawWatch, a system that searches case law and statutes to find new material pertaining to an individual subscriber's clients, areas of expertise, or other designated topics of concern.

Free trial subscriptions to the National Collection, GlobalCite, and LawWatch can be found on the Loislaw Web site. Paralegal programs and law schools that have received American Bar Association approval may receive free subscriptions to the complete Loislaw service for the use of their

STATE, FEDERAL & BANKRUPTCY PRODUCTS
FAST, ACCURATE, AFFORDABLE LEGAL RESEARCH

Loislaw

The LOIS Professional Library® Series
Loislaw offers comprehensive primary law
coverage for all 50 states, the District of Columbia,
plus 18 Federal Law Library databases.

LOISLAW NATIONAL COLLECTION℠

This comprehensive product package includes access to
Loislaw's primary law libraries for all 50 states, the District of
Columbia, and 21 Federal Law Library databases.

The Federal Law Library databases include the following:

- U.S. Supreme Court
- Rules of the U.S. Supreme Court
- The 13 U.S. Courts of Appeals
- Federal Court Rules
- U.S. Code

- Code of Federal Regulations
- Federal Register
- U.S. Sentencing Commission Guidelines Manual
- Public Laws of the U.S.

STATE/FEDERAL CIRCUIT COLLECTION℠
NATIONAL COLLECTION

All 50 states, District of Columbia, U.S. Supreme Court, U.S. Circuit Courts,
Federal District Courts, U.S. Code, CFR, Federal Register, Federal Sentencing Guidelines.

FEDERAL PACKAGE

One state, U.S. Supreme Court, U.S. Circuit Courts, Federal District Courts,
U.S. Code, CFR, Federal Register, Federal Sentencing Guidelines.

STATE AND FEDERAL

Loislaw's primary law coverage for one state and the Federal Circuit, plus
the U.S. Reports, U.S. Code and Rules of the U.S. Supreme Court.

STATE SPECIFIC PRODUCTS

Comprehensive primary law coverage in any of the
50 states, plus the District of Columbia.

STATE PRODUCTS

Comprehensive primary law coverage is available for any of the 50 states or the District of Columbia.
Please refer to the state specific collateral content for your state library.

FIGURE 12-2 Loislaw Professional Library Series. Reprinted with
permission from Loislaw product brochure, © 2001
Loislaw, Inc., An Aspen Publishers Company.

LOIS® PREMIUM PRODUCTS

LOIS® Federal District Court Opinions℠

Loislaw introduces LOIS Federal District Court Opinions.
Loislaw users can access, via the Internet, a library of selected
case opinions obtained from the U.S. District Courts.

LOIS Federal District Court Opinions include the following:

- Selected case opinions from 1932 to present. This database includes selected U.S. District Court cases cited by one of the U.S. Courts of Appeals, the U.S. Supreme Court, or one of the states' appellate courts in a final decision.
- Selected case opinions of recent cases from participating courts.
- Selected U.S. District Court Rules.

> **Visit www.loislaw.com for product specifications.**
>
> **Click on "Products & Pricing" button.**
>
> **Product descriptions appear in the**
>
> **Premium Products category.**

LOIS® Bankruptcy Court Collection℠

The LOIS Bankruptcy Court Collection
is available via the Internet.

The collection consists of the following:

- Bankruptcy Court Opinions — Subscribers can access a library of selected case opinions obtained from the U.S. Bankruptcy Courts including:
- Selected historical case opinions from 1979 to present. Additional historical cases will be added over time.
- Selected case opinions of recent cases from participating courts.
- Selected Bankruptcy Forms.
- U.S. Supreme Court.
- Rules of the U.S. Supreme Court.
- The 13 U.S. Courts of Appeals.
- LOIS® Federal District Court Opinions℠.

FIGURE 12-3 Loislaw Premium Products. Reprinted with permission from Loislaw product brochure © 1999 Loislaw, Inc., An Aspen Publishers Company.

students. Graduates may obtain subscriptions at half price if their school had a subscription to Loislaw.

Connectors

There are five connectors to use when searching for two or more words in the same field. You can mix or match multiple connectors in a search expression to make the search more specific. Use either the connector word or the symbol. A list of these connectors is as follows:

Connector	Shortcut Symbol	Searches for
AND	**&**	Both terms in the document field
OR	**_**	Either term in the document field
NOT	**%**	First term, but no term following NOT
NEAR	**/**	Both terms within 20 words of each other
NEARX	**/X**	Both times within a specified number (X) of words of each other, such as "near2"
"xx"	**"**	Two or more words as a phrase

The use of parentheses can make the search expressions even more specific. Use them to combine similar terms or to establish the order of priority when using multiple connectors. For example, using the expression

Employ near2 (terminate or discharge)

will show "employ" within two words of "terminate" or within two words of "discharge." By using the expression

(punitive or exemplary) near2 damages and bad faith

you will find either "punitive" or "exemplary" appearing within two words of "damages." The term "bad faith" will also appear in the document.

Citations

Pay close attention to the spacing and internal periods when entering the official or parallel citation number. Unlike some other systems, you should always use a space between citation segments; for example, **233 cal. r. 111** is correct. Note that the periods in the given citation are optional.

LawWatch

With LawWatch, the system will search case law, legislative acts, and databases to find new laws or articles pertaining to a subscriber's clients or specialty areas, as well as any other topics of interest designated by the user. The systeam will automatically and continuously search more than ten million pages of state and federal law and deliver the results automatically to your computer by e-mail. An on-screen tutorial will guide you through the process of setting up this system.

Special features of LawWatch include:

1. Automatic and continuous searching of more than ten million pages of state and federal law utilizing intelligent search engines

2. Results automatically delivered to your computer via e-mail or saved on your personal Loislaw start page

3. User-friendly setup—instruct with key words and activate by saving your search query

4. An on-screen tutorial that guides you through each step of the process

GlobalCite

All Loislaw subscriptions include the GlobalCite citation research service, which allows the user to scan all Loislaw databases to find documents citing the document being viewed. It will search cases, statutes, administrative regulations, and all other sources on Loislaw. The information is available in a few seconds.

Once the document has been retrieved and is open on your screen, the GlobalCite function may be performed by clicking the "GlobalCite" icon at the bottom of the page. See Figure 12-4 on pages 208 and 209 for the GlobalCite tutorial and a screen capture showing the results.

The Loislaw Web page provides links to several different categories as shown in Figure 12-5 on page 210. A simple search of all State Law Links in California yielded the results shown in Figure 12-6 on pages 211 and 212.

Unique features of GlobalCite are listed below:

1. Once you have searched a database, retrieved results, and opened the full text of the document, you will be able to cite check the document by using GlobalCite.

2. You may run GlobalCite by clicking the GlobalCite button on the bottom left of your document screen.

3. GlobalCite will search all of the Loislaw databases and provide a list of documents that cite the document you are viewing. All results will display the document name, citation, and document summary. You can hyperlink to the full text of the case by clicking on the name of the document.

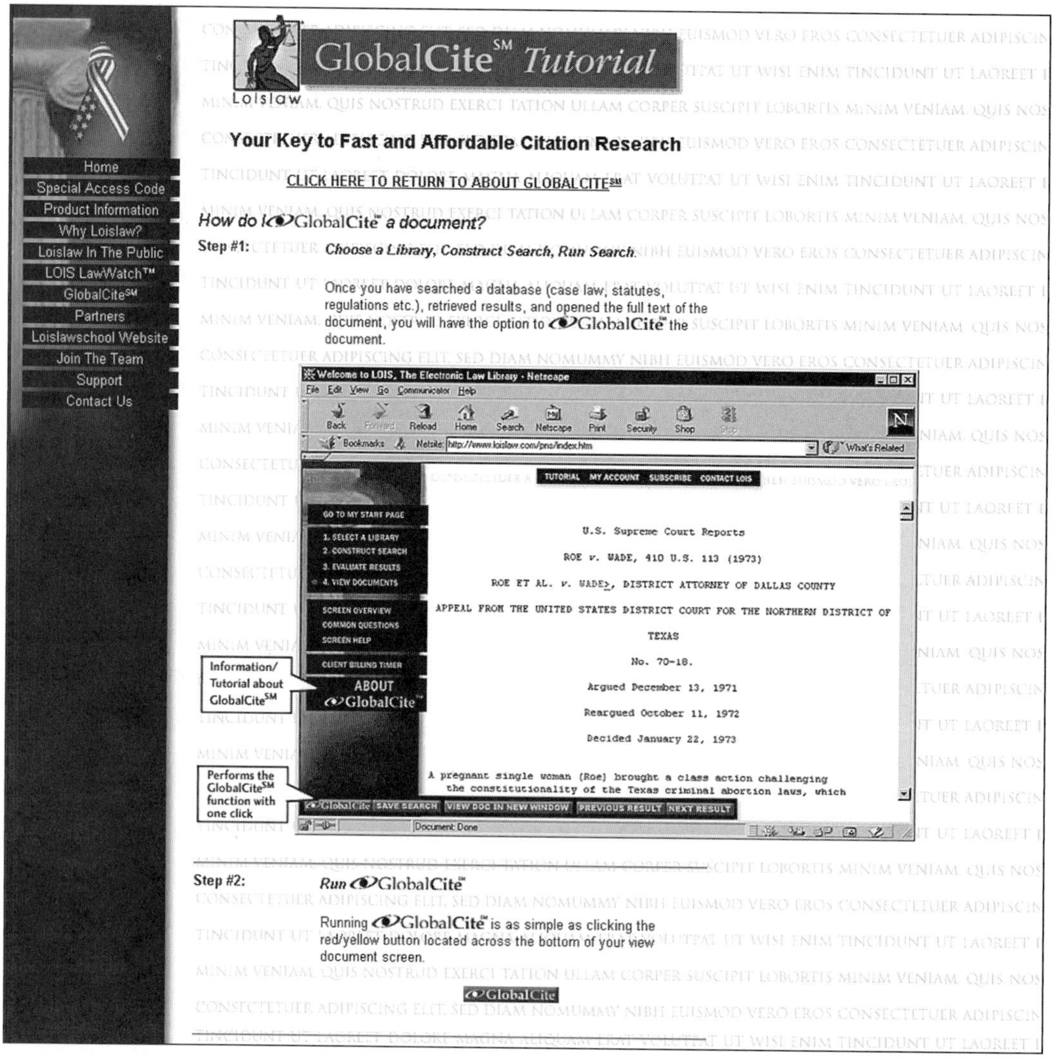

FIGURE 12-4 GlobalCite℠ Tutorial. Reprinted with permission, Loislaw, Inc., An Aspen Publishers Company.

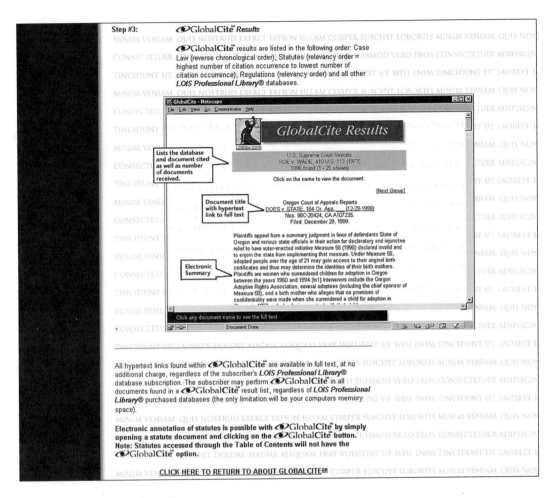

FIGURE 12-4 *(continued)*

SEARCHING IN LOISLAW

A search conducted in Loislaw can be relatively simple to accomplish. Some general steps are as follows:

1. **Start simple.**

    Start with a few terms. Do not include every possible word in your search. Choose only the most important or unique words for your topic.

FIGURE 12-5 Loislaw Web Page. Reprinted with permission, Loislaw, Inc., An Aspen Publishers Company.

California Links

Loislaw

All States' Constitution and Code

Anti-SLAPP Project

Association of Certified Family Law Specialists

Bar Association of San Francisco

CA Jury Instructions - Civil - Proposed

CA Jury Instructions - Criminal - Proposed

California Bankruptcy Network

California Bar Association

California Case Law

California Law (Counsel Connect Fee)

California Department of Justice, Office of the Attorney General

California Environmental Protection Agency --- State Water Resources Control Board

California Statutes and Acts

California Western School of Law

Cal Northern School of Law

Center For Continuing Education

Chapman University School of Law

Compex Legal Services, Inc.

Concord University School of Law

Continuing Education of the Bar California

Consumer Attorneys of California

FindLaw CLE Online

Empire College School of Law

Employment Law in California

FIGURE 12-6 California State Law Links. Reprinted with permission, Loislaw, Inc., An Aspen Publishers Company.

Glendale University College of Law

Golden Gate University School of Law

John F. Kennedy University School of Law

Links to Southern California law

Loyola University School of Law, Los Angeles

McGeorge School of Law

New College of California School of Law

Oakland County Bar Association

Pacific Coast University School of Law

Pepperdine University School of Law

Sacramento County Law Library

Santa Clara County Bar Association

Santa Clara University School of Law

Santa Cruz County Law Library

San Francisco Law School

Southwestern University School of Law

Stanford Law School

University of California at Berkeley- Boalt Hall School of Law

University of California at Davis School of Law

University of California - Hastings College of the Law

University of California at Los Angeles School of Law

University of San Diego School of Law

University of San Francisco School of Law

University of Southern California Law Center

Ventura County Bar Association

Whittier Law School

Western State University College of Law

Back to
Law Links Home

FIGURE 12-6 *(continued)*

2. Be careful with phrases.

When searching for a well-known subject like child custody, broaden your search with the NEAR operator to find all the uses of the words.

3. Use NEAR for names.

Proper names are not used consistently in the law. Therefore, when looking for a person's name or any proper name, use the NEAR connector to find all forms of that name. For example, **danielle near2 jeffries** finds Danielle M. Jeffries and Danielle Marie Jeffries.

4. Use broad terms when searching statutes, codes, and regulations.

Statute sections generally have only a few words, so be concise when searching for them. For example, **felony and murder** finds the felony murder statute.

5. Use the power of field searching.

Documents are divided into fields so you can find what you want quickly.

The Search Process

There are four specific steps for searching in Loislaw. They are described in the following list. Be sure to also use GlobalCite when appropriate.

1. Select a library.

Once you have selected the major database to search (such as California), the specific database can then be accessed (such as California Codes.)

2. Construct a search.

Figure 12-7 on page 214 shows the method of constructing a field search, which enables you to search only selected portions of all the documents in the database. The "Search Entire Document" field encompasses all of the fields for a full-text search.

3. Evaluate results.

Figure 12-8 on page 215 shows the results of a search for specific case law. These results appear in reverse chronological order. The top of the screen indicates the total number of documents that the search has retrieved and the total number

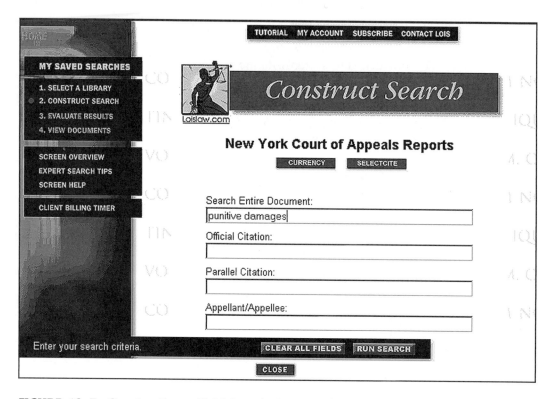

FIGURE 12-7 Constructing a Field Search. Reprinted with permission, Loislaw, Inc., An Aspen Publishers Company.

of documents that were examined. Clicking on the name of the case or heading will yield the full text of the document.

4. View documents.

Figure 12-9 on page 216 shows the full text of a document. Search terms appear in red letters with arrows at each end. Clicking on either of the arrows will jump to the next or previous search terms. Underlined blue letters (hyperlinks) show citations to case law and statutes. Click on 1 to jump to the cited document.

More comprehensive descriptions of the various parts of the Loislaw system are available online and in the Loislaw User's Guide, which is provided to subscribers. Additional information may be obtained at

http://www.loislaw.com

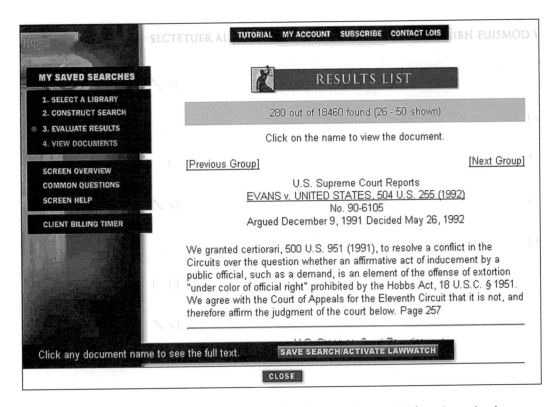

FIGURE 12-8 Results of a Search. Reprinted with permission, Loislaw, Inc., An Aspen Publishers Company.

SUMMARY

This chapter describes the many other research systems available on CD-ROM and the Internet. The Loislaw system is described in detail.

The major advantage of CD-ROM systems is their ability to hold large volumes of data. One CD will hold 300,000 pages of data. A whole series of state codes will fit on two CDs. Updates must be issued regularly, however, and it is imperative that the latest updates are always used. Attorney directories are available on CD, as well as directories of government offices and courts.

A number of document-producing software manufacturers have converted their materials to CD format. Free demonstration software packages are often available, enabling the user to try the package before making the purchase.

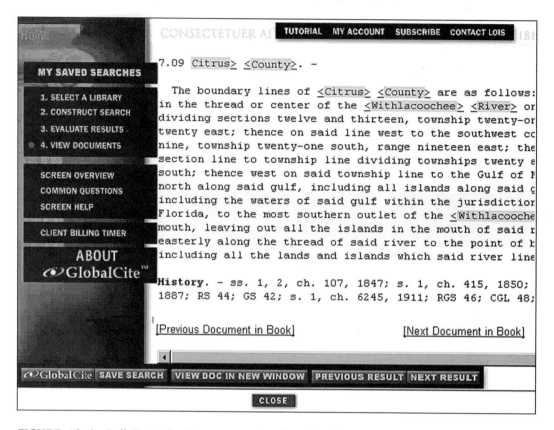

FIGURE 12-9 Full Text of a Document. Reprinted with permission, Loislaw, Inc., An Aspen Publishers Company.

The Loislaw system is a relatively new leader in the computer-aided legal research area. It provides access to over ten million documents, including both federal and state law. It represents a low-cost, high-quality legal research alternative for the legal community.

REVIEW QUESTIONS

1. Define CD research systems.

2. What are the major advantages and disadvantages of CD research systems?

3. What is Loislaw?

4. Describe the unique features of Loislaw.

5. Contrast the different updating systems for cases, including Shepardizing, KeyCite, and GlobalCite.

PRACTICAL PROBLEMS

1. Your attorney-employer has asked you to research the feasibility of purchasing a monthly subscription to the Loislaw system online. The firm specializes in bankruptcy law and uses both state and federal courts. Write a memorandum to the attorney analyzing the Loislaw system and making a determination of which of their subscription packages is best for your firm.

2. Do a GlobalCite of the *Roe v. Wade* case. Write a memorandum to the attorney discussing whether abortions are still valid in your state and under what circumstances.

address books A place to put frequently used e-mail addresses.

Auto-Cite An online citation service of LEXIS that is used to update cases and to check the accuracy of the typed citation and spellings in the case name.

bankruptcy A plan whereby a debtor who is unable to pay creditors may resolve debts by dividing assets among creditors.

CALR Computer Aided Legal Research, including using the Internet, CD-ROMs, and legal subscription services to do legal research.

chat room An online meeting room where you can meet others for purposes of discussion.

citation The identifier for a particular case, including the volume number of the book in which it appears, the series in which it appears, and its page number. For example, 8 U.S. 193 may be found in Volume 8 of *United States Reports* at page 193.

civil rights Rights of citizens guaranteed by the United States Constitution, including freedom of speech, association, and religion.

Civil Rights Acts Federal laws relating to the prohibition of discrimination based on race, color, age, sex, religion, or national origin.

Commerce Business Daily Publication that provides information about large government contracts; it lists abstracts of proposed contracts on a daily basis.

connector (W/n) Retrieves words found within a specified number of words of each other.

corporate law Area of business law that concerns the making and dissolution of corporations.

CPU Central Processing Unit: the part of the computer that processes data.

database directory A list of all databases available on Westlaw.

database identifier A code to access individual databases. For example, the database identifier for federal case law is "ALLFEDS."

databases Lists of articles on given subjects from all over the world. Provide the ability to retrieve articles from journals in the United States, Great Britain, Australia, Canada, Ireland, and New Zealand.

digest field search A search method that enables the researcher to limit the search to the law in the digest.

DOJ Department of Justice: manages the legal business of the US. Includes all federal law enforcement agencies.

DOT Department of Transportation: governs all transportation agencies of the government.

e-mail 1. (n) Electronic mail having the following parts: caption or heading, subject, copies information, body, and attachments. Also, mail that is sent via the computer and reaches its destination instantly; it can be used to send files as attachments. 2. (v) to send correspondence via the Internet.

estate planning   Preparation of wills and other estate plans for clients, probate, and the preparation of trusts.

FAA   Federal Aviation Administration: responsible for the safety of civil aviation.

family law   All types of law that deal with families, including divorce/dissolution, child support and custody, visitation, adoption, child welfare, and domestic violence.

Federal Circuit Courts of Appeal   Intermediary federal court for appeals; hears cases appealed from the U.S. district courts.

federal district courts   Trial courts on the federal level; at least one in each state.

FindLaw   A comprehensive Web site for legal sources; provides links to state statutes and cases. One of the best sites on which to find other legal resources.

FLITE   Federal Legal Information Through Electronics database includes over 7,000 U.S. Supreme Court cases from 1937–1975; includes volumes 300–422 of the *U.S. Reports.*

GENFED   General Federal library dividing the federal sources into files of primary and secondary authority.

GlobalCite   The Loislaw system for updating cases and statutes.

Graphics in Browsers   GUI (Graphical User Interfaces): used in browser programs. Represent icons or graphics on the Web page enabling you to execute commands on the computer such as scrolling or going back to the home page.

hypertext link   "Hyperlink;" connects Web pages together. Provides underlined and colored text that enable you to go to the site by clicking with the mouse on the colored text.

INS   Immigration and Naturalization Service: agency of Department of Justice responsible for admission, naturalization, prosecution of illegal entry, and deportation of foreigners.

Institute for Law and Justice   Provides links to criminal justice sites.

intellectual property   Copyright law: the right to control the copying, distribution, and performance of works, which belong to the creator or his employer.

international law   Legal relationships and interactions between countries or between individuals or corporations from different countries. International trade agreements, treaties, and contracts.

Internet   Also known as Cyberspace and the Information Superhighway. World's largest computer network connecting thousands of computers throughout the world.

Internet card catalog   Subject matter index for most sources on the Internet.

intranet   A network within an office that links members of the firm via their computers. Enables users to file their research in a central file for others' use.

KeyCite A fast method of updating a case by clicking the mouse on the case citation.

key word searches Searching by the key words that appear in a document or Web page using all words that describe the material being sought.

keyboard The part of the computer used for entering data and inputting information.

Legal Information Institute Located at Cornell University, it provides links to government agency Web pages and a large number of legal research links.

legal listserv Discussion group dealing with legal issues; available at **http://www.kentlaw.edu/lawlinks/listservs.html.**

legal pad A site providing a large collection of links to law-related sites as well as legal clip art for insertion in documents.

Legal Research Law Link The American Bar Association's link to branches of government, courts, Judicial Council, court home pages, law school libraries, and other legal reference sources.

LEXIS A computerized legal research system.

LEXSEE A system on LEXIS that enables you to find a case if you have its citation.

Lexstat A method of searching for federal statutes on LEXIS when you know the title and section number.

listserv Subscription to e-mail on a given topic. Once registered, all mail sent out to the listserv is received by the subscriber.

Loislaw A computerized legal research system using either the Internet or CDs.

manual research Research using books from the library but not computer systems.

Martindale-Hubbell Directory An attorney directory for all states in the United States.

MELVYL A large online catalog with records of over ten million holdings in libraries in the University of California system.

modem An internal computer device that allows computers to communicate using a telephone line.

monitor The part of the computer that displays the output from the computer; it looks like a television screen.

mouse A pointing input device attached to the computer and used to move the cursor on the computer screen in order to open and close files, enter programs, and enter commands.

newsgroups International bulletin board with many topics and conversations available.

NTSB National Transportation Safety Board: provides information about airline accidents and incident reports. Responsible for investigating airline accidents.

primary sources Primary authority that is binding, including laws, statutes, cases, administrative regulations, and other like sources of law.

real property law Litigation relating to real estate transactions and landlord/tenant law.

Restatement of Law Books published by the American Law Institute describing the law in a general area and how it is changing.

root expander The use of the "!" symbol to find all forms of a word.

search engines Web sites that provide a list of categories on which you can search. Examples are Yahoo, Gopher, and Veronica.

SEC Securities and Exchange Commission: administers federal and state laws that regulate the sale of securities.

secondary source Persuasive authority that is not binding such as restatements, articles, encyclopedias, and treatises on the law.

secretary of state Oversees the State Department. Chief foreign affairs adviser.

Shepardizing Updating cases and statutes by creating a list of relevant cases and other material that occurred after a case was handed down from the courts and that has a direct bearing on that particular statute or case. Using a *Shepard's* citator to trace a case or statute's history after the case has been decided by the court. Done instantaneously on LEXIS by transmitting the citation preceded by the word "shep."

State Department Provides advice on foreign policy and negotiation in foreign affairs, issues passports, negotiates treaties, assures protection of United States interests in foreign countries, supervises immigration laws abroad, and provides travel advisories in foreign countries.

table of authorities service Enables the researcher to find all other cases citing the instant case. Shows any significant negative history.

Terms & Connectors A method of searching using pre-defined terms and connectors for writing issues.

treatise A comprehensive volume on a legal topic.

URL Uniform Resource Locator: the Web address of a page on the Web.

"update" hyperlink A system enabling the researcher to see legislation that either amends or repeals a statute.

West Legal Directory Biographical listings of over one million lawyers.

Westlaw A computerized legal research system.

Westlaw Bulletin (WLB) A database providing a brief description of recent state and federal cases.

Westmate Special software used to connect to the Westlaw system.

WIN (Westlaw is Natural) Using natural language to conduct a key word search.

INDEX